THE OUTDOOR PLAYSPACE
naturally
FOR CHILDREN BIRTH TO FIVE YEARS

Editor
Sue Elliott (Dip KTC, B Sc Hons, M Sc)

Pademelon Press

First published 2008 by
Pademelon Press
7/3 Packard Avenue
Castle Hill, New South Wales, 2154

Reprinted July 2008

Editing and Project Management by Persimmon Press
Design and Production by tania edwards design
Illustrations by Sharyn Madder
Index by IndexAT
Printed in China through Bookbuilders

The outdoor playspace naturally for children birth to five years.

ISBN 9781876138271 (pbk.).

1. Play environments - Australia - Planning. 2. Day care
centers - Australia - Landscape architecture. 3. Child
care services - Environmental aspects - Australia. 4. Play
- Australia. I. Elliott, Sue. II. Title : Outdoor play space naturally.

712.70994

Foreword

We could never have loved the earth so well if we had had no childhood in it.

George Eliot
The Mill on the Floss

The Outdoor Playspace Naturally—For Children Birth to Five Years is written by people who love the earth and want young children to love it as well. For many of us, especially those raised with good access to the outdoors, there is a straight line between outdoor happiness as a child and adult love and concern for the natural environment. Going further, noted Harvard scientist EO Wilson formulated the 'biophilia hypothesis' stating that because we evolved in the outdoors we are hard-wired or genetically disposed to love life—people, animals, plants (Wilson, 1993).

Julie Davis and Sue Elliott describe, in their well-researched Introduction, how many children in the developed world have much diminished access to the outdoors, especially natural areas. Very young children dependent on their carers are especially at risk. How will these children learn to love the world?

The chapter authors lay out the case for richly natural playspaces in early child-hood centres. The superbly illustrated pages provide authoritative information on child development, safety, cultural resonance, inclusion, curriculum, design, and community development. There is also a chapter on natural playspaces in Denmark, England, and New Zealand, emphasising the sociocultural basis of what we provide for our children.

The graphics are especially persuasive. Looking at the dozens of photographs showing centres with rocks and stones, logs, water features (even a creek), chicken pens, lizard habitats, prickly bushes, hiding places or cubbies, gardens, steep places, one has to think—why can't our centre be like that? The collective wisdom of the early childhood experts authoring the chapters acknowledges dangers but offers precautions—for example, sunscreen and copious shade for UV radiation; preventative lotion and mindfulness for ticks; awareness of spiders, snakes and possums; attention to uneven and sharp places.

Perching places for adults are also explicitly mentioned and shown—if the adults aren't comfortable, outdoor time loses out. Appealing line drawings illustrate important arguments—the bubble wrapped child is an apt symbol of our fearful era.

The case is made for children's wholesome development, for environmental sustainability, for community building and sustaining playspaces. It is also evident that these playspaces are relatively cost-effective. The case studies

< iii >

showed A$50 000 as the most expensive playspace while others using much volunteer labour and existing features had very low expenses. By contrast, a large public 'playground improvement' project in one American city had a price tag of US$100 000 per playground—mostly for manufactured equipment and surfacing.

From the case studies, the reader may also notice that a thriving, plant-rich playspace takes years of sustained effort. Sue Humphries at Coombes School in England, for instance, started developing her exemplary beautiful school-yard in 1971 and still keeps her hand in. One of the problems in the US with schoolground naturalisation is the rapid turnover in school and centre leadership. US private early childhood centres seem to have a better time of it, especially when owner-operated or a parent cooperative.

Once when I was visiting a schoolground in England, a small child proudly pointed out to me a 12 foot (3.6 metre) strip of grass at the edge of the asphalt, backed by a row of bushes, backed by a high brick wall: 'That's our wilderness.' The unlimited range of children's imaginations and their sweet ability to make much of little is striking. This publication well illustrates many small touches that can be applied almost anywhere for children's enjoyment and learning.

I very much enjoyed my time with this book. Although the Australian biome is not like most of North America, early childhood people in many places, such as in the American Southwest, would be able to directly utilise many ideas, especially on water conservation techniques. Others in this country and elsewhere can adapt its principles. I especially value the book's bright confident spirit.

We can give young children substantial experiences in natural environments that will resonate into their adulthoods. The year 2007 was the 100th anniversary of Rachel Carson's birth. The founder of the modern environmental movement, Carson passionately believed that children should interact directly with the natural world, not only for immediate interest and delight, but also because such interactions would sustain children's innate 'sense of wonder', and make this sense of wonder:

> … so indestructible that it would last throughout life, as an unfailing antidote against the boredom and disenchantment of later years, the sterile preoccupation with things that are artificial, the alienation from our sources of strength (1965).

The Outdoor Playspace Naturally guides us to creating the environments and relationships that can fulfill Carson's vision.

Mary S Rivkin Ph D
Associate Professor
Early Childhood Education
University of Maryland, Baltimore County, USA
16 September 2007

References

Carson R, 1965, *Sense of Wonder*, HarperCollins, New York, p 43.

Wilson EO, 1993, 'Biophilia and the Conservation Ethic', in SR Kellert and EO Wilson (Eds), *The Biophilia Hypothesis*, Island Press/Shearwater, Washington, DC, pp. 31–2.

< iv >

Contents

< v >

Preface

This publication has arisen from concerns shared by the editor and contributing authors about children's playspaces in early childhood services in Australia. Over recent years we have informally collected anecdotes and observed the changes in children's playspaces to the point that we can no longer simply lament these concerns, but must do something about them! This publication is an attempt to publicise our concerns and offer guidance and information to early childhood educators, centre coordinators, management committees, designers and all those involved in the provision of early childhood services. The contents of this publication will be challenging for those addicted to quick fix playspace solutions and glossy catalogues. The focus is very much on collaboratively creating natural playspaces that evolve over time and have significant meaning for each successive generation of children. Increasing urbanisation, concerns about children's health and wellbeing and disconnection with nature suggest that the time is right to instigate change in outdoor playspaces.

As editor, it did not take long to convince my colleagues that it was time to put our concerns and thoughts in print. I sincerely thank them for their trust in me as a first-time editor to work on this publication. The chapter authors willingly shared their knowledge and expertise both in writing and discussion over the pre-publication year. My thanks to them for their dedication to the task and to their families and workplaces for understanding and support.

A particular thank you to the case study subjects in Chapters 8 and 9 who led the way in demonstrating playspace design and affirming the value of natural playspaces for children in early childhood centres. The information they have provided will no doubt inspire, challenge and provoke others.

The chapters of this publication are well illustrated both with photographs and graphics. So much about natural play spaces can be communicated visually and the photographs are a source of inspiration. Thank-you to the staff, parents and children who contributed to the playspaces depicted in the inspiring photographs throughout the publication. Also, thanks to Neil Bayley Hume City Council, Patti Morgan Knoxfield Kindergarten, Justine Mason Christchurch College of Education New Zealand, Rosemary Hillier Berwick Kindergarten, and Kidsfirst Kindergartens Christchurch New Zealand who provided additional photographs. Thank-you to Sharyn Madder who captures the essence of natural outdoor play spaces in her graphics.

Thank you to Pademelon Press for taking the opportunity to publish this work and their able editing and design work.

Lastly, thanks to my family, Phillip, Katie and Andrew, their support for mum's projects is never ending!

Sue Elliott

< vi >

Author profiles

Barbara Champion (TITC Frankston and GDIESE Melbourne)
Barbara is the Executive Director of the Playgrounds and Recreation Association of Victoria (PRAV). She began work at PRAV in 1998 following a history of employment in the education and local government sectors in Victoria. Her experience includes leadership and/or involvement in a number of community-based education, arts and health organisations. Barbara is the Chair of the Australian Standards on Playgrounds Safety and supports the work of PRAV across all areas.

Julie Davis (Dip Teach, B Sc (Envir Studies), M Envir Ed, PhD)
Julie is a lecturer in the School of Early Childhood, Queensland University of Technology, teaching in the curriculum areas of Studies of Society and Environment and Health Education. Her passion is early childhood education for sustainability, demonstrated by her co-founding of the Queensland Early Childhood Environmental Education Network in 1996. Recently she has been conducting research into how sustainability principles and practices become embedded into schools and early childhood settings. She is co-author with Sue Elliott of *Early Childhood Environmental Education: Making It Mainstream*. Currently Julie is working towards the development of a national approach to research for early childhood education for sustainability.

Sue Elliott (Dip KTC, B Sc Hons, M Sc)
Sue has worked in a variety of early childhood settings and lectured at the tertiary level in early childhood training courses. She shares a passion for environmental education and science education in her teaching. Sue is co-author of several books including *Snails Live in Houses Too, Environmental Education for the Early Years* and *Just Discover Connecting Young Children with the Natural World* and author of *Patches of Green*, the first review of early childhood environmental education in Australia. Currently, she lectures at RMIT and convenes the Australian Association for Environmental Education Early Childhood Special Interest Group.

Michelle Hocking (Dip KTC)
Michelle is a kindergarten teacher with experience in a variety of early childhood settings including extended hours and sessional kindergarten, mobile preschool and funded kindergarten in a long day care setting. She has written and conducted early childhood programs for the Royal Botanic Gardens Melbourne Education Service, Melbourne Aquarium and the Melbourne Museum Children's Museum. She is currently employed at the Coburg Children's Centre, Melbourne, as the Program Planning Co-ordinator and is a past Convenor of the Melbourne-based organisation Environmental Education in Early Childhood Vic. Inc. She has a passion for nature based playgrounds in early childhood settings.

< vii >

Mary Jeavons (MLArch and AILA member)
Mary is a Registered Landscape Architect with around 20 years experience in the design of children's environments of all kinds. She is a keen observer of children and her work reflects a desire for children to engage with the landscape as active participants. Mary is the director of Mary Jeavons Landscape Architects, a division of Jeavons & Jeavons Pty Ltd. This firm specialises in the design of school grounds, secondary colleges, public parks and custom designed playgrounds, early childhood centres and other settings, including therapeutic and play spaces in hospitals, BMX tracks, and even a children's cemetery. The firm has a major focus on the design of play and recreation facilities accessible to children and adults with disabilities and also prepares municipal strategy plans for playgrounds, open space, and leisure and sports facilities, in association with @leisure, a sister firm.

Ric McConaghy (B Arts, Adv Dip Fine Art)
Ric has previously managed the South Australian Department of Recreation and Sport Playground Unit and is now an independent playspace consultant across Australia. In recent years he has been involved in the planning and design of playground projects from major regional playspaces to community-based childcare centres. He prepared the South Australian Local Government *Playground Manual* and edited the 1997 *Kidsafe Playground Manual* in New South Wales. He is an active speaker for Kidsafe, the Standards Australia Association, PRAV and a Councillor at Large for the International Play Association. He aims to raise enthusiasm and to empower communities to create exciting, diverse and secure naturalistic playspaces that do not rely solely on structures, but incorporate art and design elements.

Kerry Rogers (Dip KTC, B Ed)
Kerry has a long standing involvement with preschool programs both as a hands-on teacher, trainer and consultant specialising in outdoor play and environments. Her teaching experiences have included semi-rural, metropolitan and inner urban areas as well as in the demonstration program at the Melbourne Lady Gowrie Child Centre. She has been responsible for coordinating both federally and state funded in-service training programs as well as presenting training sessions and keynote addresses at many conferences. She has also been involved in the training, assessment and mentoring of students from a range of tertiary training institutions.

Joanne Sørensen (B Ed (EC))
Joanne is an early childhood teacher in a multi-age centre on the grounds of Queensland University of Technology, Kelvin Grove, run by the Creche and Kindergarten Association of Queensland. Joanne has a strong interest in environmental education, which is reflected in her daily practices. Joanne has had extensive involvement with Danish students on international practicum at her centre and she has also visited Denmark to learn about their early childhood practices and environments.

Sue Vaealiki (M EnvEd, DipT, KDip)
Sue has been involved in early childhood teaching for over 25 years, as a teacher, manager, lecturer and now as a Programme Leader at the Te Tari Puna Ora o Aotearoa/New Zealand Childcare Association in Wellington, New Zealand. As a teacher and a manager, Sue was involved in creating and supporting teachers to design outdoor playspaces. Sue has a Masters of Environmental Education through Griffith University and has previously been

< viii >

involved in developing and delivering 'Education for Sustainability' courses for student teachers at Christchurch College of Education. Sue also has a strong interest in teacher education and regularly facilitates environmental workshops and seminars for early childhood teachers.

Tracy Young (Dip Soc Sci, B Ed Ch Dev, Grad Dip Ch Dev)
Tracy has worked in the early childhood profession for many years in child-care centres and kindergartens. Tracy has no formal science qualifications, although she has always had a passion for animal welfare and environmental education. Tracy believes that an enthusiasm for science and nature studies can be passed on though creative teaching and removing some of the mysteries that surround science. She actively implements this approach in her current role lecturing at Swinburne University in Melbourne. Tracy has co-authored several publications with Sue Elliott exploring topics such as connecting with nature, demystifying science and technology experiences for young children and exploring natural outdoor playspaces. Tracy is currently enrolled in postgraduate research and her thesis will explore connections with the natural world and the implications for early childhood educators and children.

< ix >

Introduction

Why natural outdoor playspaces?

Sue Elliott and Julie Davis

In a country where the outdoor lifestyle of bush and beach is iconic, it is a paradox that the next generation is increasingly cooped up indoors or playing in synthetic outdoor playspaces—places where there is not a tree to climb, a cicada nymph shell to discover or a mud pie to be moulded. Is this what we want for our children?

This publication is a response, in particular, to the emergence of synthetic and generic outdoor playspaces in early childhood centres in Australia. The authors are concerned from a number of perspectives. These include young children's opportunities for exploration, discovery and learning; the physical and mental health of children and staff; human connections with nature and the promotion and practise of sustainable living. This publication brings together a group of authors with expertise in early childhood playspace use and development, children's health and wellbeing, landscape architecture, playspace standards and sustainability. We are committed to change, to shifting the paradigm about what early childhood outdoor playspaces should look like. *The Outdoor Playspace—Naturally* will inspire early childhood educators, managers of children's services, parent committees and others in the early childhood sector to reflect critically on what is currently happening in our early childhood centres and to actively participate in the paradigm shift towards natural outdoor playspaces.

Where have we come from? Once upon a time ...

Once upon a time, educational theorists such as Froebel, Dewey and Rousseau espoused the importance of learning outdoors in natural settings for children. Froebel (1782–1852), often described as the father of the kindergarten movement, saw analogies between the work of educators and gardeners, envisioning kindergartens as gardens for children where close contact with nature was fundamental to children's education. Rousseau (1712–1778) saw 'the natural environment as a vehicle for freeing the spirit of children' (Gutek, 1968, cited in Roopnarine and Johnson, 1993, p 3) and a fundamental source of education. Somewhat later, Dewey (1859–1952) lamented the industrial revolution and its impact on children, suggesting that the school surrounded by natural environments was the way forward. For Dewey 'good schooling ... was dependent on the outdoor world, because that is where life occurs' (Rivkin, 1998, p 200).

Recently, such views of childhood and children's learning—originating from developmental psychology—have been strongly critiqued by post-structuralist theorists and educators, represented by writers such as Burman (1994), Cannella (1997) and Mac Naughton (2003). These theorists have done much to reshape and reconceptualise thinking and practices in early childhood, focusing attention particularly on the roles of gender, race, class and disability in children's learning and development (Lambert, 1995). Similar attention, however, has not been directed at analysing children and their relationships with nature or natural elements. While the idea of children growing up as free spirited, joyful, independent beings in a Garden of Eden 'at one with nature' in the care of nurturing early childhood 'gardeners', now seems rather old-fashioned, this lack of analysis of the relationships between children and nature has meant that power differentials between humans and non-humans have not been questioned in the early childhood education field. This absence perpetuates the (socially constructed) hierarchy of humans over other living beings and, therefore, that nature and natural elements exist essentially for human use and should be exploited. Perhaps this derives from the understandably anthropocentric or human centred world-view one would expect from sociologists and social theorists. Nevertheless, the failure of post-structuralists to consider relationships between humans and the natural world means that there are 'equity blind spots' in post-structuralist thinking.

One such 'blindspot' relates to how people interact with other species and natural elements; for example, how do early childhood educators and children treat the resources of nature around them? Are insects, spiders and snakes simply pests to be destroyed or removed because they may impinge on human wellbeing? Are cats and dogs privileged over possums and lizards because they are domesticated; that is, they have learned to coexist with humans? Because water play is so good for so many areas of young children's learning, does this mean that water should be used as if there are no limits to its availability?

A second 'blind spot' relates to post-structuralism's failure to address issues of intergenerational equity, even though post-structuralist perspectives have, at their heart, the 'struggle for social justice' (Canella, 1997, p 157). At its broadest level, sustainability means living in ways that do not reduce the choices and life prospects of future generations—our children, grandchildren and other descendants. A significant aim of sustainability is for each successive generation to share equitably in the resources of this planet. We are already living in a world where environmental conditions are damaged and diminished, threatening the Earth's life-support systems, and it is children and future generations for whom the implications are most profound. If, through our current actions as early childhood educators, we fail to understand that caring for the Earth as well as caring for people needs to be a central tenet of our beliefs and actions, one wonders what future generations will think of us. One might ask, *What kind of ancestors will we be?*

When one considers that Dewey was concerned about children's access to outdoor playspaces post industrial revolution, and that the situation is far more dire now, it would appear that there needs to be a reconceptualisation of thinking about children, play and nature that goes beyond the naïve beliefs of the developmentalists, but addresses the omissions of the post-structuralists.

What's happening now?

The need to rethink the theoretical bases of early childhood education is urgent from two perspectives. There is the increasingly limited access to outdoor playspaces which impacts on children's health and wellbeing, and the generic synthetic outdoor playspaces now emerging that are potentially alienating children from nature.

Rivkin (1995, p 2) states 'children's access to outdoor play has evaporated like water in sunshine'. As habitats for wildlife are vanishing under increasing urbanisation and population, so too are children's places for outdoor play. Just a generation ago there were creeks, open spaces, streetscapes and bushy areas that local children could claim as their own and could play in from dawn to dusk. In addition to local open spaces disappearing, 'the average Australian house block has shrunk by 15% in the past decade, but the average house size has increased by 15%' (Hoban, 2005, p 8). Supported by indoor entertainment and electronic media, the focus for children appears to have moved significantly from outdoors to indoors for play. In agreement, Louv (2005) cites a child questioned about their preference for indoor or outdoor play; the answer: 'Indoors, because that's where the power points are!' Other factors contributing to decreasing outdoor play opportunities include the busy-ness of children's lives. There is no time to 'just play', according to Honore (2004), fuelled by media-generated perceptions about safety and risk (Furedi, 2001). An interweaving of all these factors has contributed to both the evaporation of outdoor play opportunities and significant change in the types of opportunities available for children today.

Shrinking outdoor playspaces—where can children play?

In our experience, these changes are reflected in the memories that early childhood educators share about their childhood experiences of play. Older early childhood educators remember their local playspaces with a great sense of meaning and connectedness, while younger educators find this challenging and turn to more structured, predictable indoor play memories. The memories we carry are described by Chawla (1990, p 18) as 'radioactive jewels buried within us, emitting energy across the years of our life'. They reach well beyond childhood to impact on adult lives and can be a resource to draw upon when developing outdoor playspaces and programs for young children. Unfortunately, if the current trend towards indoor play continues, there will be fewer and fewer 'radioactive jewels' to inspire and fuel early childhood educators.

Additionally, reduced access to outdoor playspaces is a factor—along with diet—that can be linked to high levels of childhood obesity. Currently, 25 per cent of Australian children are overweight or obese (Hoban, 2005, p 8) and various programs are now being implemented to promote physical activity outdoors from 'walking school buses' to organised sports in after school services. A further answer lies in ensuring easy access to safe and inviting local playspaces in early childhood settings, schools and communities generally.

Beyond access to outdoor play, the type of outdoor playspaces promoted by the early theorists were 'gardenlike' or 'natural', not the synthetic generic outdoor playspaces increasingly evident today in early childhood centres. Why have these types of sterile playspaces emerged? There are many answers ranging from perceived safety concerns, to adult needs for order and tidiness, to glossy play equipment manufacturers' catalogues, to simply a lack of understanding and valuing of outdoor play. After all, according to many adults, the real work of learning occurs indoors (and preferably at desks)! The following pages attempt to define a natural playspace and to identify the advantages that such spaces offer young children in early childhood centres.

What is a natural outdoor playspace?

A review of the literature reveals a variety of words and phrases to describe a natural outdoor playspace, each one lending a particular interpretation.

Greenman's (1988, p 177) work is well recognised in the early childhood sector. He refers to environmental play yards 'which encourage interaction with plants and animals, water, dirt, weather and the lifecycle'. He states that such play yards 'offer children education at its most compelling'. Thus, a natural playspace is one that invites or compels children to interact and, potentially, create meaning and a sense of place out of their surroundings.

In their research about the learning potential of different types of outdoor playspaces, Herrington and Studtmann (1998) contrast landscape-based and equipment-based or 'placeless' playspaces. They have defined the landscape-based playspace to include natural materials such as stepping-stones; unmown grass, sensory plants and landforms such as plant-generated vegetative rooms or enclosed spaces and grassy mounds. Both elements—the natural materials and the landforms—are essential to a natural playspace.

According to Elliott and Davis (2004, p 5) the natural outdoor playspace can be described as 'a sea of natural sensory stimuli'. Particularly for children in urban areas, a natural playspace provides both diverse and different sensory experiences that, amongst other benefits, promote children's sensory development. Young and Elliott (2005) refer to 'environmental playspaces' and focus on the potential for environmental education in early childhood centres where the outdoor playspace has a variety of natural elements. More telling are their various references to the generic synthetic type of playspaces as 'dead spaces', 'McDonald style playgrounds' and 'eye-candy playspaces'. Surely we can do better than this for the next generation?

In Scandinavia, the notion of a natural outdoor playspace has been taken a step further with the establishment of '*Naturbornehaver*' or nature nursery schools where children play in woodlands and meadows. As Adhemar (2000, p 44) describes, it is a 'startlingly simple concept of taking children out in nature as often as possible, for as long as possible, in all weathers and in all seasons'. Sorenson in Chapter 9 explores this concept fully, but for the purposes of defining a natural outdoor playspace, it can be interpreted that the total amount of time spent outside all year round is important. Without time all year round, opportunities to explore the changing elements of a natural playspace are profoundly limited.

In summary, a natural outdoor playspace:

- reflects the local landscape and climate, though may be a reconstruction of the indigenous environment;
- is dominated by natural elements; for example, trees, shrubs, sand, soil, flowers;
- invites open-ended interaction, exploration and manipulation;
- provides opportunities for risk-taking, spontaneity and discovery;
- stimulates the senses in all respects;
- is alive and unique;
- is accessible at all times and in all weathers;
- promotes a sense of place for children and adults;
- contains multiple 'habitats' within the overall space;
- promotes a sense of wonder; and
- is always evolving and never finished.

Why natural outdoor playspaces?

As authors, researchers, educators and playspace designers, we are convinced about the fundamental importance of natural playspaces for children. However, there are many in the early childhood sector with no appetite for risk or challenge who would view such a playspace as too difficult or even inappropriate. The following paragraphs provide a rationale for early childhood educators and others to advocate for natural playspaces for young children. We believe natural playspaces can be justified in terms of play opportunities and potential, physical and mental health benefits for children and adults, enhanced connections with nature and the promotion of sustainability. For each particular early childhood centre the rationale employed may differ, for some centres it may be multifaceted and incorporate all of the supportive points noted above. For other centres, just one locally relevant point maybe enough to shift the prevailing paradigm about the most desirable outdoor playspace.

A place of opportunities and potential

Opportunities for exploration, discovery and learning for young children are significant in natural outdoor playspaces. The 'aliveness' of a natural outdoor playspace ensures that, with each new day, there are new discoveries for children. It might be the caterpillars in a tree, the changing colour of leaves or the types of visiting birds; all provide a focus for children's innate curiosity. In the hands of early childhood educators who are sensitive and empathetic to both children and the natural environment, these discoveries become rich learning opportunities—not only about particular species, their habitats, food needs and lifecycles, but also about the systems that inextricably connect humans and the natural world and the skills for exploring these connections.

An opportunity for bird observation.

Research about the impact of natural outdoor playspaces on children is limited, however several research papers provide some significant insights into the potential of natural outdoor playspaces for children.

Herrington and Studtmann (1998) researched the developmental impact of landscape-based and equipment-based playspaces in early childhood services. Their research indicated that the equipment-based playspaces promoted primarily physical development, while landscape-based playspaces promoted learning in a range of areas including physical, social, cognitive and emotional. The broader focus for learning promoted by landscape-based playspaces also impacted on the social hierarchy in the groups of children at play, such that physical prowess was no longer the only factor determining the social hierarchy. In addition, the landscape-based playspace with defined pathways—for example, stepping stones—promoted topological and positional understanding of the playspace; and its vegetative rooms—the bushy cubbies—supported a sense of place.

Vegetative rooms, bushy cubbies, dens or enclosed spaces have been the focus of several researchers (Kirkby 1989; Kylin 2003). Kirkby (1989) contrasted young children's play in purpose-built, adult-built cubbies with bushy cubbies. She observed that children's play was more sustained, complex and creative in the bushy cubby type. The bushy cubby, like a theatre stage, provides multiple entrance and exit points, a setting that promotes more complex scenarios than a one-door purpose built cubby. The materials or props used in the cubbies differed too. Bushy cubby play tended to rely on whatever was at hand for children to improvise with creatively. These loose parts for play might be leaves, twigs or seedpods found in the cubby space, while the purpose-built cubby play was determined by the materials usually placed in the cubby by staff. How often do we see these materials—such as tea sets, tables and chairs—used in our early childhood centres, thus dictating, in subtle ways, what the play scenario is to be? Bushy cubbies are more likely to promote the diverse types of play that are most beneficial to children's development.

A bush cubby.

Kylin's (2003) research was with primary school age children who created dens in their local neighbourhoods. Nevertheless, elements of this research are just as relevant to early childhood services. Kylin (2003) identified that the character of the landscape and the materials available impacted on the potential for den building. Landscapes with a variety of spaces, both open and enclosed, a variety of vegetation and a variety of loose materials for building were the most inviting. From the child's perspective the den is also a secret and social place. 'The common factor in the experience of the den as a social and secret place is the sense of control that children feel they have, both over the den as a physical space and over the other children who share the den' (Kylin, 2003, p 21).

The natural playspace provides a wealth of opportunities, not just simply for exploration and discovery, but as a stage with in-built props for promoting diverse and creative play.

Physical and mental health

There is no doubt that both natural and synthetic playspaces promote physical health, but there are some subtle advantages to be recognised in natural playspaces. Natural playspaces are more likely to provide a variety of terrain and ground surfaces to challenge children's physical skills. Walking variously on grassy mounds, tanbark, soil, gravel, stepping stones or rocky creek beds demands sensory integration and appropriate physical skill responses not required by monocultures of synthetic surfacing. Natural playspaces often incorporate purchased moveable climbing equipment pieces, but are not dominated by large fixed equipment that tend to lose physical challenge for children over time, which they then utilise in 'riskier' ways to create new challenges. In addition to the flexibility that moveable equipment promotes in a natural playspace, natural elements can also provide different types of physical challenge. A tree to climb, a bushy thicket to navigate through and a trickle stream to jump across—what more inviting physical challenge could a young child want?

A trickle stream to jump across!

There is also increasing research interest in the enhancement and improvement of mental health through exposure to natural spaces. Have you ever wondered why the window seat in a city office building is prized, why living near a park adds value to your real estate, or why it just feels good to sit in a leafy green space? Humans are craving vegetated spaces in our increasingly urban environments. Kaplan and Kaplan (1989) propose that 'leafy green spaces' have a restorative effect on the human brain that allows us to return refreshed to focus on our tasks. Attention restoration theory suggests that leafy green spaces require only involuntary attention and engage us without effort (Kaplan, 1995). The defining criteria applied by Kaplan and Kaplan (1989) to restorative places are: a sense of fascination and curiosity; a sense of being away from usual settings; a sense of being part of a larger whole; and, compatibility with an individual's needs. These criteria can equally be applied to natural outdoor playspaces. Adhemar (2000) supports the positive effect of natural outdoor spaces on mental health, reporting reduced stress levels and greater enjoyment of work among Danish early childhood educators working in nature nursery schools.

Wells (2000) and Taylor, Kuo and Sullivan (2001a; 2001b) have considered the effect of leafy green spaces specifically on children. Wells (2000) found that children in inner neighbourhoods exposed to leafy green places demonstrated higher attention levels, while Taylor, Kuo and Sullivan (2001a) found they demonstrated greater self-discipline. In the latter research, the children were simply able to view such spaces from their windows. Imagine the potential benefits if they were also able to play in them! Taylor, Kuo and Sullivan (2001b) also collated parents' behaviour ratings of children with Attention Deficit Disorder in indoor settings, and also in leafy or non-leafy outdoor settings, and found that the children's symptoms were most relieved in leafy outdoor settings. Thus, there may well be significant behavioural benefits for children if natural playspaces are provided. In turn these benefits impact positively on staff and on children's learning potential.

Mental health benefits may also be created by natural playspaces through developing a sense of place and a sense of identity. On a large scale, humanity is, perhaps irrevocably, damaging the planet. On a smaller scale, in natural outdoor playspaces, children can create a sense of place and identity without causing irrevocable damage. Natural playspaces, by definition, can be manipulated and changed by children and, in so doing, a sense of ownership, a sense of place, and understanding of oneself in relation to others and of the playspace, emerges. Hart (1987, p 224) states 'because, unlike the world of people, the physical world does not itself change in response to a child's actions, but simply reflects his or her manipulations, it offers a particularly valuable domain for developing one's sense of self'. For children 'the physical qualities and characteristics that can be planned and designed contribute only a small part of the whole that provides a total experience of space' (Chawla, 1992 in Kylin 2003, p 4).

Children's sense of place is often symbolic and contrasts with the adults' physical perceptions of space. Kylin (2003) asserts that children describe a space in terms of activity and meaning, whereas adults will describe the physical or cognitive parameters. The conflict between these perceptions comes to the fore when children's much-loved secret and enclosed bushy play corners—where imaginary dinosaurs or fairies might lurk—are perceived as difficult to supervise and maintain, dangerous and problematic, or even wasted spaces according to early childhood educators. At times, such conflict is compounded by adult-directed programming that denies or limits children's voices and their participation in planning their educational experiences. Acknowledging these differing perceptions is fundamental to developing and working with children in a natural outdoor playspace in order to create a sense of place, identity and belonging.

Connecting with nature

Human survival for thousands of years has depended on intimate daily contact with the natural environment and it is only in very recent human history that industrialisation and urbanisation have removed this daily connection. Evolutionists would argue that while the physical spaces we inhabit have changed, fundamentally humans still desire contact with nature and it is essential to our deeper psychological needs and wellbeing. 'Quite possibly, then, human beings retain a neurological and even a psychological need for the natural environments in which they evolved' (Partridge, 1984, p 126). E.O. Wilson (in Kellert and Wilson, 1993) refers to this innate connection with nature as 'biophilia'. It is evident that biophilia pervades human behaviour everyday from our affinity with water to preferences for natural spaces over built spaces.

For how long, though, will 'biophilia' permeate human behaviour? Kahn and Kellert (2002) caution that with each successive generation the benchmark changes. Nature is redefined and we are becoming increasingly removed from nature. They refer to this phenomenon as 'generational amnesia'. The risk of generational amnesia is significant if early childhood educators and others do not seize the opportunities in the early years to foster intimate and meaningful connections with the natural environment.

Early childhood is often described as a unique and critical time for connecting with nature (Wilson, 1996; Carson, 1998 originally published 1956; Tilbury, 1994). Nature connections made in childhood are instrumental to the construction of values, development of an 'ecological self', and can be viewed as a lifelong resource. But, under what circumstances do these connections materialise? While much of the research has focused on adult reflections of childhood, it is frequently cited that both direct contact with nature and the influence of other adults as mentors, intrepreters and role models are funda-mental (Chawla, 1988).

Louv (2005) has coined the phrase 'nature deficit disorder' to describe children who have become alienated from nature. Their relationship with nature is a superficial one only realised through various media, and through classroom lessons about rainforests, not via a personal relationship involving direct experience. One cannot imagine a child with nature deficit disorder demonstrating care or concern for nature when they have never been directly immersed in nature.

A natural outdoor playspace ensures that there are opportunities for children to realise their connections with nature while developing 'the uniquely human skills of tool making, problem solving and decision making ... In order to develop in the right ethical direction, they must be rooted in childhood opportunities for fully experiencing the Earth and for understanding the influence of humankind upon it. How will we learn to live collaboratively with the planet otherwise' (Moore, 1986, p 23).

Sustainability

We live in an era of uncertainty, instability and rapid change that presents both major challenges and profound opportunities. Children growing up in the twenty-first century will live their entire lives in change, with their experiences of environments—social, cultural, virtual and natural—being very different from those of just one generation ago. While children's choices may seem endless, there is mounting concern about the consequences of lifestyles that focus on materialism, individualism and nature-conquering technologies, while ignoring social disparities, social cohesion and human processes that marginalise natural systems (Davis and Elliott, 2003). As the Worldwatch Institute (2000, para 25) warns 'Nature has no reset button'. Increasingly, it is being recognised that the way humans are currently living is unsustainable, and that what is necessary is a transition from an unsustainable society to a sustainable one, while there is still time.

Sustainability, however, cannot be readily grafted onto the economic, social and political practices that have caused the problems in the first place. It requires learning how to live in dramatically different ways that recognise both human and ecological dimensions of development. Deep-seated cultural change is necessary involving both our lifestyles and our core values—a transition to thinking and practices that are infinitely more ecocentric than at present. We all need to consider the long-term consequences of how we live so that we all 'live lightly *on* the Earth' and 'live lightly *with* the Earth'.

While not the complete answer, education 'must be a vital part of all efforts to imagine and create new relations amongst people and to foster greater respect for the needs of the environment' (UNESCO, 1997, p 15). However, given the scale of the challenges, it is necessary to make fundamental changes to education —including early childhood education—so that the transition to sustainability is not delayed.

Education for sustainability (EfS) needs to be a 'new vision of education that seeks to empower people of all ages to assume responsibility for creating a sustainable future' (World Summit on Sustainability, 2002). This is characterised by holistic, interdisciplinary educational frameworks that help humans and human systems work with and within Earth's ecological systems—a very different orientation that stresses community, capacity building and creativity rather than control, fit and dependence (Sterling, 2001).

Education for sustainability will not be effective, however, without consideration of the environments in which learning and living takes place. Malone (2004, p 56) cites recent research that shows that, no matter where in the world children live, they have similar wishes:

> They want clean water and enough food to eat; they want to be healthy and have the space to learn, develop, and play; they want friends and family who love and care for them; they want to participate in community life and be valued; they want to collaborate with adults and make the world a better place for all; they want peace and safety from threats of violence; they want access to a clean environment where they can connect with nature; they want to be listened to and their views taken seriously.

These simple wishes—articulated by children and for children—are a request for environments in which children have positive futures and, embodied in these desires, lie the guiding principles for sustainable living. Natural playspaces must be a central feature of such environments, reversing the trends towards sanitised, 'safe', structured outdoor playspaces with regimented games and inflexible play equipment, or the movement indoors towards technologised play. As Thomas and Thompson (2004, p 21) state, 'This generation, more than any other before, will need the environmental awareness and citizenship that is instilled through exploration of the natural environment in childhood'. This is important because, as Dighe (1993) emphasises 'One can hardly imagine a generation of persons with neither interest in nor knowledge of the outdoors making responsible decisions regarding the environment' (p 62).

If we provide synthetic outdoor playspaces that cannot be shaped by children, what will they grow up knowing and feeling? Natural outdoor playspaces can be continually shaped by each successive generation of children that plays in them.

Conclusion

The following chapters provide early childhood educators, managers of children's services, parent committees and others in the early childhood sector with the inspiration and knowledge to develop natural playspaces in early childhood centres. In Chapters 1 and 2, Ric Mc Conaghy identifies the design principles and processes that underpin a natural outdoor playspace. Tracy Young in Chapter 3 takes the reader a step further with details about natural features to be incorporated in outdoor playspaces. Playspaces are designed to meet the needs and interests of a diverse range of ages and abilities and both Kerry Rogers in Chapter 4 and Mary Jeavons in Chapter 6 specifically address these points. In Chapter 5, Barbara Champion reconciles the need for safe, but challenging, playspaces in relation to Australian Standards while in Chapter 7, Michelle Hocking employs layers of complexity to approach the natural playspace from the planning perspective of the early childhood educator. The final two chapters focus on case studies. Chapter 8 provides cases in Australia while Chapter 9 looks overseas. These inspiring examples illustrate the potential for natural playspaces and identify exemplary practice.

The aim of this book, then, is to encourage adults to develop natural playspaces, as *landscapes for children to embroider with the loose threads of nature*. In such landscapes, children can create meaning, develop a sense of place, connect with the natural world and feel empowered to live healthy, sustainable lives. As Sobel (1990, p 12) states 'If we allow people to shape their own small worlds during childhood, then they will grow up knowing and feeling they can participate in shaping the big world tomorrow.'

References

Adhemar A, 2000, 'Nature Schools', *Resurgence*, Number 199, March/April, p 44.

Burman E, 1994, *Deconstructing Developmental Psychology*, Routledge, New York and London.

Cannella G, 1997, *Deconstructing Early Childhood Education: Social Justice and Revolution*, Peter Lang Publishing, New York.

Carson R, 1956 reprinted 1998, *The Sense of Wonder*, Harper and Row, New York.

Chawla L, 1988, 'Children's Concern for the Natural Environment', *Children's Environments Quarterly*, Vol 5 No 3, pp 13–20.

Chawla L, 1990, 'Ecstatic Places', *Children's Environments Quarterly*, Vol 7 No 4, pp 18–23.

Chawla L, 1992, 'Childhood Place Attachments', in I Altman and M Setha, Eds, *Human Behaviour and Environment: Advances in Theory and Research, 12: Place Attachment*, Plenum Press, New York and London.

Davis J and Elliott S, 2003, *Early Childhood Environmental Education: Making It Mainstream*, Early Childhood Australia, Canberra.

Dighe J, 1993, 'Children and the Earth', *Young Children*, Vol 48 No 3, pp 58–63.

Elliott S and Davis J, 2004, 'Mud Pies and Daisy Chains: Connecting Young Children and Nature', *Every Child*, Vol 10 No 4, pp 4–5.

Furedi F, 2001, 'Making Sense of Parental Paranoia', Retrieved 02/11/05 from http://www.frankfuredi.com/articles/parenting-20010425.shtml.

Greenman J, 1988, *Caring Spaces, Learning Places: Children's Environments that Work*, Exchange Press, Redmond, WA.

Hart R, 1987, 'Children's Participation in Planning and Design' in C Weinstein and T David, Eds, *Spaces for Children: The Built Environment and Child Development*, Plenum Press, New York and London.

Herrington S and Studtmann K, 1998, 'Landscape Interventions: New Directions for the Design of Children's Outdoor Play Environments', *Landscape and Urban Planning*, Vol 42, pp 191–205.

Hoban R, 2005, 'The Bubble Wrap Generation', *Vic Health Letter*, Issue No 24 Summer pp 8–13.

Honore C, 2004, *In Praise of Slow*, Orion, Great Britain.

Kahn PH and Kellert SR, 2002, *Children and Nature*, The MIT Press, Massachusetts, USA.

Kaplan S, 1995, The Restorative Benefits of Nature, *Journal of Environmental Psychology*, Vol 15, pp 169–182.

Kaplan R and Kaplan S, 1989, *The Experience of Nature: A Psychological Perspective*, Cambridge, New York.

Kellert SR and Wilson EO, 1993, *The Biophilia Hypothesis*, Island Press, Washington DC.

Kirkby M, 1989, 'Nature as Refuge in Children's Environments', *Children's Environments Quarterly*, Vol 6 No 1, Spring pp 7–12.

Kylin M, 2003, 'Children's Dens', *Children, Youth and Environments*, Vol 13 No 1, Retrieved 20/01/04 from http://cye.colorado.edu.

Lambert B, 1995, 'A Post-structuralist Analysis of Learning in Early Childhood Settings', in M Fleer Ed, *DAPcentrism: Challenging Developmentally Appropriate Practice*, AECA, Canberra.

Louv R, 2005, *The Last Child in the Woods. Saving our Children from Nature Deficit Disorder*. Algonquin Books, USA.

Mac Naughton G, 2003, *Shaping Early Childhood; Learners, Curriculum and Contexts*, Open University Press, UK.

Malone K, 2004, 'Holding Environments: Creating Spaces to Support Children's Environmental Learning in the 21st Century', *Australian Journal of Environmental Education*, Vol 20 No 2, pp 53–66.

Moore RC, 1986, *Childhood's Domain*, Croom Helm, Kent England.

Partridge E, 1984, 'Nature as a Moral Resource,' *Environmental Ethics*, Vol 6, pp 101–30.

Rivkin M, 1995, *The Great Outdoors: Restoring Children's Rights to Play Outside*, NAEYC, Washington.

Rivkin M, 1998, 'Happy Play in Grassy Places: The Importance of Outdoor Environment in Dewey's Educational Ideal', *Early Childhood Education Journal*, Vol 25 No 3, pp 199–202.

Roopnarine JL and Johnson JE, 1993, *Approaches to Early Childhood Education*, 2nd ed, Prentice Hall, New Jersey.

Sobel D, 1990, 'A Place in the World: Adults Memories of Childhood's Special Places', *Children's Environments Quarterly*, Vol 7 No 4, Spring pp 5–13.

Sterling S, 2001, *Education and Learning in Change*, Green Books, Bristol, UK.

Taylor A, Kuo F and Sullivan W, 2001a, 'Views of Nature and Self-discipline: Evidence from Inner City Children', *Journal of Environmental Psychology*, Vol 21, pp 1–15.

Taylor A, Kuo F and Sullivan W, 2001 b, 'Coping with ADD: The Surprising Connection to Green Play Settings', *Environment and Behaviour*, Vol 33 No1, pp 54–77.

Thomas G and Thompson G, 2004, *A Child's Place: Why Environment Matters to Children*, Retrieved 20/7/04, from http://www.green-alliance.org.uk/publications/PubAChildsPlace_page195.aspx.

UNESCO, 1997 (Dec 8–12), *Educating for a sustainable future: A transdisciplinary vision for concerted action*, Paper presented at the International Conference on Environment and Society: Education and Public Awareness for Sustainability, Thessaloniki.

Wells N, 2000, 'At Home with Nature Effects of "Greenness" on Children's Cognitive Functioning', *Environment and Behaviour*, Vol 32, pp 775–9.

Wilson R, 1996, 'The Development of the Ecological Self', *Early Childhood Education Journal*, Vol 24 No 2, pp 121–3.

World Summit on Sustainability, 2002, Chapter 36, Agenda 21, *Basis for action*, A 36.8, UN Department of Economic and Social Affairs: Division for Sustainable Development. Retrieved on the 13/12/2003 from: http:// www.un.org/esa/sustdev/documents/agenda21/english/agenda21chapter36.htm.

Worldwatch Institute, 2000, *Information economy boom obscuring Earth's decline*, Retrieved 16/2/2000, from http://www.worldwatch.org/ alerts/000115.htm.

Young T and Elliott S, 2005, 'Environmental Education: Connecting with Nature', in E. Dau Ed, *Taking Early Childhood Education Outdoors*, Tertiary Press, Croydon.

Designing natural playspaces:
principles

1

Ric McConaghy

Introduction

The lives of children have become increasingly organised and structured over the last decade. Children are escorted from early childhood centres and schools to gym or sport and to music or dance lessons. The amble past neighbouring houses, a free-wheeling bike ride or a public transport adventure to and from early childhood centres and schools have been largely replaced by the dash in the four-wheel drive to the drop-off zone. Play is one of the last instances of unstructured, non-specific experimental activity that children engage in. And the adult response has largely revolved around the installation of playground structures with fairly prescribed activities.

The facilitator of the natural playspace seeks to provide a place where linkages are formed between the child and other children, the child and his/her environment and the child and his/her carers. But, it is also a place that provides a theatre for the child's imagination. A theatre where children may direct their own experiences, create and initiate their own rules of engagement and have a broad range of opportunities that extends beyond just the physical.

Playspace models

Historically, children have played wherever they could, and often in the most dire circumstances. In the early twentieth century specific places for public play became more common. With the advent of improved technology, the focus for children's play in the second half of the twentieth century shifted to the provision of play equipment. Fixed play structures appeared in early childhood centres, schools and local parks. By the mid 1980s in Australia, a desire grew to complement the abundance of play structures with other elements that gave a balance of experience to the play opportunities. The desire was particularly strong in the early childhood sector where limited resources and limited space was being dominated by purchasing and installing the latest and greatest physical activity structure.

As one response to this changing trend, Crocker, McConaghy and Miers (1989), at the Playgrounds Unit of the Department of Recreation and Sport in South Australia, developed a collaborative model of education and information dissemination through personal visits to early childhood centres throughout the state. From that grew the Playspace Model that was intended to act as a reminder of the basic elements required to create a complete playspace incorporating a balance of play experiences. Interlocking circles were used to depict the playspace so that each element was neither valued or devalued more than any other, but all contributed equally and linked to indicate the complementary usage between elements.

A similar model was later proposed by Walsh (1991) in her well regarded reference *Early Childhood Playgrounds: Planning an Outside Learning Environment*. The model by Walsh (1991) involved three interlocking circles of quiet, active and open types of playspaces and placed emphasis on the delineation between types of playspaces to minimise intrusion—a significant point which is explored through natural playspaces in this publication. Moore, Sugiyama and O'Donnell (2003) have recently contributed to model development with the 'CPERS scale' for physical environments based on Piagetian principles. Their model describes the early childhood centre as a place of many functions and physically groups these functions into modules around common core or shared facilities within the centre. One module might be a defined space for a

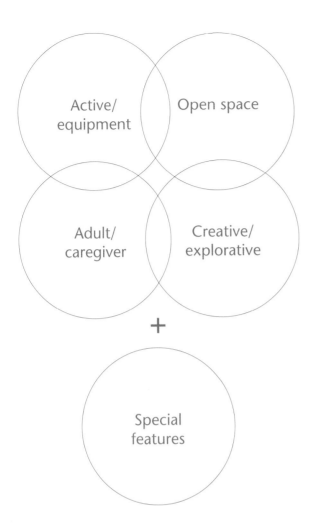

Active/
equipment

Open space

Adult/
caregiver

Creative/
explorative

+

Special
features

*Playspace model developed by
Crocker, McConaghy and Miers
(1989).*

particular group of children and within the module can be found designated
house keeping areas for beds, meals or toilets and activity areas for play.
The CPERS scale permits rating of the early childhood centre according to
13 sub-scales grouped under four headings of A. Planning, B. Building as a
Whole, C. Indoor Activity Spaces and D. Outdoor Spaces, each sub-scale
containing multiple assessment criterion. Of the total 143 assessment criterion
applied, only 15 are identified under D. Outdoor Spaces. The CPERS scale
relates to the entire indoor and outdoor physical environment with a primary
focus on indoor built elements rather than outdoors and, therefore, has limited
use for the purposes here. We are now endeavouring, through this publication,
to make the outdoor playspace a primary focus.

Key design elements

Based on the above discussion of playspace models, the following key design
elements can be identified:

- active/equipment;
- open space;
- creative/explorative;
- early childhood educator/adult; and
- special features.

Active/equipment

Fixed or portable equipment offers many play experiences and has been a focus of play provision for some time. Desirable equipment experiences include swinging, sliding, spinning, springing and scrambling or climbing. All equipment should be designed and installed to be sympathetic to the local landscape, conform to the Australian Playground Standards (refer Chapter 5) and cater for the play needs of the age group utilising the space. The play equipment industry has become increasingly sophisticated and there are many people just a phone call away who are more than willing to take potential clients through a full range of products. There is a current trend toward removing fixed equipment from early childhood centres and developing open spaces with impact attenuating surfaces for use with portable equipment which can be changed on a daily basis to suit the program.

Portable equipment—the variety and change possible with portable equipment makes it preferable to the fixed equipment option.

Open space

Open space provides a flexible area for a variety of play experiences ranging from ball games to tumble mats, block building and dramatic play. A strategically located open area can also be a vantage point from which both staff and children can survey the playspace for inviting play opportunities. Open space is a critical design element and must be declared on a design drawing. If it is not declared it may be perceived by some as empty space and the natural inclination will be to fill it. Many a desirable fragment of open space in primary schools has been lost to the invasion of the temporary classroom, car park or the insertion of the mandatory rock with commemoratory plaque. In many early childhood centres, the same problem occurs when a centrally located large fixed climbing structure, or even a well intentioned but ill-placed multi-poled structure or tree for shade, ensures that no open flexible space is possible.

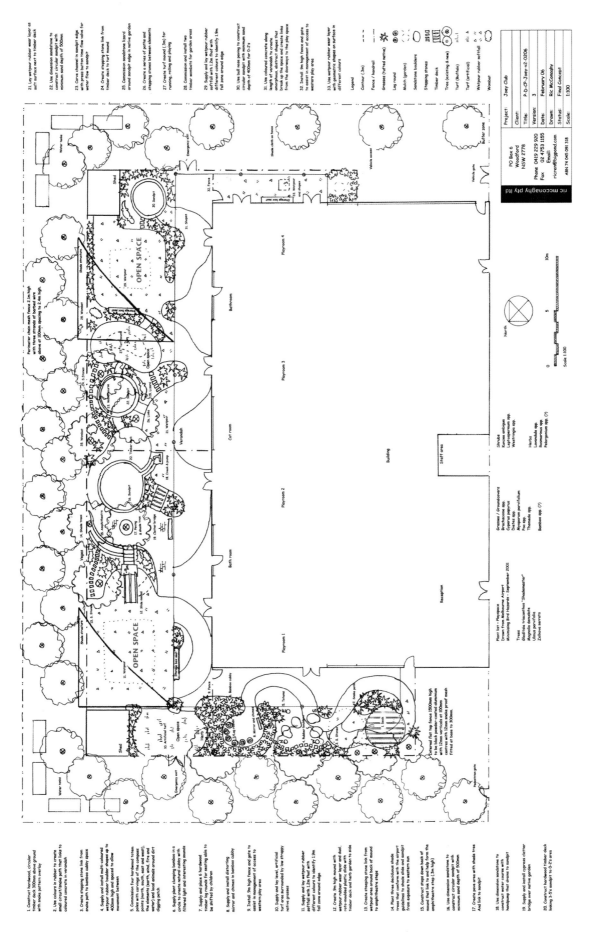

Ensure that open space is not filled in by writing 'OPEN SPACE' on the drawn plan.

A simple arrangement of tiles adds aesthetic interest and invites creativity.

Determine the best place for open space in terms of ease of supervision, appropriateness for the intended ground surface type and access for maintenance vehicles. Once determined, then write in large friendly letters 'OPEN SPACE' on the drawing and give an indication of the desirable extent of that space. It is not possible to specify a desirable size as every site has its own topographic parameters, management issues and usage patterns. Perhaps it is best to suggest that some is better than none, and more is better still. Be mindful that areas of rubber surfacing without equipment and unencumbered hard paved areas can provide some open space, but are not ideal.

Creative/explorative

The creative/explorative element is an essential aspect of a space for children's play. Various items can be incorporated to reflect this element such as sandpits, water courses, textured planting and rock formations (further items to inspire creativity and exploration are detailed in Chapter 3). These items readily invite and encourage imagination and symbolic play and support the broad range of aspirations and abilities that children bring to a place for play. Exercise is needed not only for the body, but also for the mind, imagination and spirit.

Early childhood educator/adult

Supervision—landscape elements can be introduced throughout the space to allow for easy supervision and comfort.

Early childhood educators and other adults will take children outdoors based not just on what is there for the children, but also in relation to how comfortable they themselves are, how easy it is for them to supervise the children and how easy it is to set up play experiences. The design of a children's playspace needs to consider the adult users too (refer Chapter 7).

Special features

Special features is such a broad topic that it will be more thoroughly covered in Chapter 3. Essentially, these features will include artistic elements, cultural and ecological references/installations, contextual thematic elements, animal enclosures and sensory elements. They are important in linking the playspace with both the users and the local community and enhancing the diversity of play opportunities.

Lizard—small sculptures of various materials can engage children to interact with local flora and fauna.

Spiral sandpit—sandpit with water bubbler and channel to sand surrounded by open planting. There is also a movement activated bird sounds element.

Underlying design principles

The following list of principles is provided to ensure that the concept design of a playspace gives due consideration to the diversity of children's play needs:

- access to a range of experiences;
- balance of opportunity;
- ecology and indigenous planting;
- children's cultural references;
- linkages/connectivity; and
- space.

Hopefully it also provides a launching point for extensive discussion within the community and collaboration as to the aspirations of all those who provide, manage and use the playspace.

Access to a range of experiences

There needs to be substantial consideration of access to a wide range of experiences for the diversity of children who may use the playspace. It is crucial that access is considered in broader terms than just providing physical access to a particular place within a site. Access can be interpreted in many ways at both macro and micro levels, but has historically resulted in a focus on making provision for wheelchairs. Statistics vary, but the percentage of people with a disability in Australia who make use of a wheelchair is generally less than

5 per cent of the population of people with a disability. Wheelchair access does provide a good measure of physical access to a certain point. However, ramps often provide little more than a higher vantage point to view others playing, whilst still not providing opportunities for participation or experience.

Consequently, providing access carries greater responsibilities than simply meeting gradient ratios and installing conforming handrails. For example, access may mean incorporating textured surfaces for vision-impaired children or quiet leafy retreats for respite during challenging times. For further details refer to Chapter 6.

Balance of opportunity

Provision for children's play has manifested in many ways over the years. An evolution from simple private games such as marbles and hopscotch to public provision of sophisticated, specialised equipment has highlighted much about how we as a community seek to understand and make provision for children and children's play.

A drive through most suburbs in Australia will reveal that the focus for children's play provision for some time has been play equipment and this is also reflected in early childhood centres. There is certainly a place for play equipment in children's spaces, but it is equally imperative that there is a balance of provision that complements the equipment and offers more diverse play opportunities.

Equipment provides opportunities for development of gross motor skills and other physical competencies as well as giving opportunity for decision making and risk, and some degree of socialisation, sharing and collaboration. Elements worthy of consideration to complement equipment include open space, landscape elements such as slopes, diverse predominantly indigenous planting, a range of loose materials, sand and water, intimate spaces, interactive sculptural pieces, sound and quiet spaces. These complementary elements offer opportunities for less competitive play and more social and collaborative play, role play, interaction with the environment and loose parts, quiet spaces and places for retreat, explorative spaces. Such elements can invoke a sense of wonder and intrigue.

Ecology and indigenous planting

The term natural is applied to spaces that endeavour to make provision for more than the active play opportunities provided by manufactured equipment. However, the changes wrought by increasing urbanisation make it arguable that even the most heavily planted spaces are no longer natural; simply because of the degree of intervention required to establish a landscaped space. Thus, the term natural is tenuous. The point, though, is to endeavour to create a space that reflects many aspects of the local environment and illustrates the valuing of a range of materials beyond just metal and plastic. Materials could include mulch, rocks, timber, soil, sand and living plants.

The use of indigenous plants not only gives context but, because they occur in the area naturally, they have a high probability of success and will require only reasonable maintenance once established. Furthermore, indigenous plants attract local animals, both large and small and offer considerable climate modifying opportunities that have many advantages over structures.

Shade structures can be both effective and make a bold and immediate architectural statement, but they can also be expensive to purchase and maintain

and will deteriorate over time. Trees are cheaper to establish and just get better over time. The budget usually allocated for shade structures will buy an enormous amount of plant material, and will even allow for the purchase of super advanced stock, so an effect can be just as immediate as a shade structure. The balance of money between what is spent on trees opposed to what would be expended on shade structures can be used to create other play opportunities (refer Chapter 5 for further detail).

Children's cultural references

The increasing consideration of art elements in playspaces is desirable, but it is necessary to ensure that this provision is informed by and relevant to children. There is little that is less edifying than a vast and expensive construction that is accompanied by a long-winded plaque explaining the many intrigues that give the element meaning to the artist. Layers of meaning and sophistication are to be encouraged, but not to the point where the play experience is diminished and the meanings are all but inaccessible to the intended users. Finding a balance between spelling-it-out and secrecy is the aim.

Using properly organised and facilitated art workshops can be an excellent way to create both ideas and actual elements to be included in the playspace that give it local cultural references appropriate to the community. For example, families can work on clay tiles for use in a construction process or Indigenous artists can be engaged to work with the children to create referential artwork of local significance and accessibility. Siting of the artwork in the playspace at the children's level and in places where it may become a play focus is essential.

*A mosaic ball invites exploration
and sensory discovery.*

Linkages/connectivity

The overall playspace can be viewed as a pattern of linkages or connections and these can provide spatial awareness cues or simply entice the user in a multiplicity of directions. The access ways and pathways are obvious links between play areas and buildings, but there are more subtle links. Visual linkages using patterns of plant material or introducing art or landscape architectural elements can suggest new places to explore or journeys to take. For example, materials such as bamboo or scented and under-pruned Melaleuca shrubs are

A native New Zealand pukeko bird sculpture created at Mount Pleasant Kidsfirst Kindergarten in Christchurch, New Zealand, has become a focal point for play. A parent, Diane Jamieson, worked for a term with the teacher, Angie Dalley, and the children to create the pukeko from papier-mâché. Later, it was covered in fibreglass and re-painted to protect it from the weather and prolong its unique presence in the playspace.

great to create a planted tunnel pathway. Secret seating places under pergolas create opportunity for connecting with space, while verandahs with concertina doors can be a transitional or linkage space between indoor and outdoor areas.

Space

Blessed as we are in Australia with the impression of vast space we are sometimes a bit blithe in our provision of space for outdoor play. The increasing pressure on space, particularly in urban areas, schools and early childhood centres, means that designers and educators must be more vigilant ensuring sufficient space remains on the agenda for children.

Space is necessary for creating the balance of opportunity previously mentioned. Current state regulations for early childhood centres should be viewed as the minimum space and these regulations apply irrespective of the age of the child—babies and toddlers need outdoor space too! Wherever possible, the space per child should exceed the regulatory requirements, which in most states of Australia is 7 square metres per child although it is 5 square metres per child in New Zealand—double this would be a good start.

In conclusion, the challenge for early childhood educators and playspace designers is to keep at the forefront these underlying models and principles to ensure the best possible outcomes for children. The following chapter builds on this initial chapter and guides the reader through the process of playspace design.

The pathway creates linkages, while plants, rocks and tiling add further interest.

References

Crocker P, McConaghy R and Miers T, 1989, 'Creating natural playspaces' *in South Australian Recreation Institute Conference Proceedings*, South Australian Recreation Institute, Adelaide.

Moore GT, Sugiyama T and O'Donnell L, 2003, 'Children's physical environments rating scale' in R Cornish ed, *Children the Core of Society, Proceedings of the Australian Association for Early Childhood Biennial Conference*, CD-ROM Paper 73, Canberra.

Walsh P, 1991, *Early Childhood Playgrounds: Planning an Outside Learning Environment*, Pademelon Press, Castle Hill, NSW.

Bibliography

Ceppi G and Zini M, Eds, 1998, *Children, Spaces, Relations: Metaproject for an Environment for Young Children*, Reggio Children and Commune di Reggio Emilia, Italy.

Goltsman SM, Iacofano DS and Moore RC, Eds, 1987, *Play for All Guidelines: Planning, Design, and Management of Outdoor Play Settings for All Children*, MIG Communications, USA.

Greenman J, 1988, *Caring Spaces, Learning Places: Children's Environments that Work*, Exchange Press Inc., Redmond, USA.

Moore RC, 1990, *Childhood Domain: Play and Place in Child Development*, MIG Communications, USA.

Author unknown, 2004, Play Inclusive Action Research Project (P.inc), *Inspiring Inclusive Play Handbook*, The Yard, United Kingdom.

Designing natural playspaces:
processes

Ric McConaghy

2

What would you like in your playspace?

Introduction

The design process proposed here will assist with determination of the appropriate location and organisation of the intended playspace as well as offer encouragement for an inclusive design process. The word 'community' is employed below in the broadest sense possible to include children, families, early childhood educators, committees of management, property owners, the neighbourhood and relevant auspicing or regulatory bodies.

Preparation of a brief

The capacity for any designer to realise the aspirations of a community will have its foundation in the preparation of the brief. The brief should declare the intent of the project, the specific aspects that need to be addressed, the expected outcomes, a list of clear deliverables, the proposed timing of each stage and a definitive budget figure. The brief should also make clear the regulatory requirements and the process of selection for submitted tenders.

Ultimately, the brief should indicate to the designer the approach that the client wants to take and the outcomes they expect. This will allow the designer to undertake a full assessment of the commitment required and to establish a methodology and fee proposal that will deliver the project within budget and on time.

The brief should include the following sections:

- background;
- rationale;
- design objectives;
- design principles;
- general requirements;
- detailed requirements;
- proposed budget;
- timeline;
- consultant's role; and
- deliverables.

Background

A basic description of the site and its environs including location, boundaries, previous history and usages, surrounding activities, local demographics, the number and ages of the children attending and the hours of centre operation.

Rationale

The intent of the project must be clearly stated in terms of the aim of commissioning the project. Put simply, why has the project been instigated? The rationale may include reference to the centre philosophy and other considerations pertinent to the particular client.

Design objectives

This includes how the site will be used after the development and what the design should accommodate to achieve the design objectives. The objectives might relate to the type of play experiences desired, effective supervision, linkages between areas and amenities such as water access, storage etc.

Design principles

What regulatory acts, best practice guidelines, standards and licensing requirements need to be met in order to constitute a conforming design? This information varies from state to state and must be checked locally.

General requirements

This includes an explanation of the intent of the client to deliver a certain type of development.

Detailed requirements

An opportunity for the client to be specific in their demands which will inform what inclusions and exclusions may constitute a conforming tender.

Proposed budget

The budget identifies the monetary figure available for construction of the project and defines what expenditure will be included or excluded from the figure such as design fees and documentation. Some centres may prefer to use volunteer labour for some elements to reduce cost and facilitate community engagement.

Timeline

This declares critical check points during the process that will need to be met in order that the project proceeds according to the requirements of the client; in particular, expenditure parameters and centre program operation considerations. Sometimes project timelines need to fit with periods of centre closure or less busy times of the year.

Consultant's role

This defines what is expected of the designer and who is responsible for programming the project, marketing, ancillary services, documentation and facilitation of meetings, stakeholder consultation etc.

Deliverables

What is expected at each stage of the project including the number of drawings, format of drawings, opinion of probable costs, project reports and any other documentation required.

Selection of a designer

It is common practice to include in the brief the process of selection for submitted tenders and, particularly, the weight of each item in the submitted tender. Items of significance will include a demonstrated understanding of the brief, acceptable timing, competitive fee, previous projects of a similar nature, conforming to tender requests, suitable references and, possibly, performance in a final interview. Identifying these items of significance will allow the potential designers to structure their submission in a way that will better meet the client's needs.

In selecting a designer, the following general considerations may also be helpful. A designer must have understandings of the concepts discussed below.

Early childhood playspaces

A very clear understanding of the early childhood centre's program, philosophy and aspirations for the space available are critical. Early childhood outdoor playspace design is a very specific design field and the outdoor playspaces are often small and heavily populated with active children. With only 7 square metres per child as the norm this demands a space that is well-organised, easily maintained and totally useable by young children and adults.

Legislated requirements

A strong understanding of the state or federal government departmental requirements and other licensing agencies relevant to early childhood services is required. Also, familiarity with the Building Code of Australia (BCA) to construct a suitable transition from the indoor to the outdoor space and the Australian Standards for Playground Equipment and for All Abilities Access (Refer Chapter 5) is important.

Process and materials

A strong understanding of the processes of construction for the playspace, particularly for large projects with multiple tasks to be undertaken over a designated time frame and requiring multiple skills. Knowledge of the diversity of materials available for playspace construction and reputable local suppliers of such materials is also relevant.

Communication

Most importantly, very good listening skills as well as being a very clear communicator are essential. There is a very broad range of people with whom the designer will need to communicate including children, staff, parents, clients, government agencies, contractors and suppliers. To keep the project moving along in a collaborative manner, effective and appropriate communication is critical.

Site selection

A range of priorities, possibilities and politics influence the siting of new early childhood centres. These include local demographics, public transport and planning policies. Unfortunately, the potential for a natural outdoor playspace is often well down the list of considerations and the site for the centre may have been prescribed by the planner or developer.

It is worth considering the type of playspace required by the local community prior to selecting a site, if at all possible. Some sites will be better suited to a structured style of outdoor playspace whilst others will better suit natural spaces. Better still, a combination of order and chaos will meet more needs. In Australia, a north facing aspect is desirable for the outdoor playspace as this promotes sunlight in the playspace and the use of landscape designed plantings helps to control the micro climate. However, it is also important to consider the need to create green refuges in heavily built up urban areas. Older inner urban early childhood centres with well established trees could be an oasis for inner urban children whose outdoor play opportunities at home are limited.

Sloping sites can create opportunities and interest. These boulders create challenging steps with pockets of planting.

Site analysis

Prior to design, the community must develop a sense of the location and how the outdoor playspace sits within its surrounds and in relation to service buildings. A site survey prepared by a registered surveyor is an essential starting point. The site survey will cover boundaries, existing entrances, existing buildings, existing vegetation (including spot levels), contours at 200 mm intervals, existing services (power, water, taps), orientation, scale (preferably 1:100), existing drainage provision and all other physical elements of the site that may influence the design.

Items to be observed during the initial site inspection and to be noted on the initial base plan include any other elements not previously included on the plan that may have an influence. This sort of information typically comes from someone with an ongoing familiarity with the site and could include elements such as areas that always stay damp, overly shady/sunny areas, typical prevailing winds, dead spots that children don't use, and places prone to influence from outside the boundary (for example, excessive noise, traffic).

Other elements for the designer to consider in consultation with the community are discussed below.

Underground and overhead services

Not only does this help you locate various elements within the space, for example, lighting and taps, but it is imperative to establish the location of all services prior to construction in order to avoid costly mistakes during construction.

Orientation

It is critical to know where the sun will be during the day and what variations will occur over the full range of seasons to assist in the placement of shade and

A water pump is a useful feature, but its location should be determined after checking the plumbing and considering the location of sand and digging areas.

also to ensure there are some sunny areas. The amount of direct sun or shade will vary significantly according to geographic location, topography and the presence of mature trees, so a localised assessment approach is required. A shade study of the playspace site may be a useful way to quantify the shade available during daily and yearly peak ultraviolet radiation times, further regional information and advice can be obtained from The Cancer Council Australia or state-based Cancer Councils (Refer Chapter 5).

Scale

It is imperative somewhere on the drawing to include not just the scale ratio, but also a drawn scale rule. During the consultation process, the plans will often pass through many hands and can often be reproduced and distributed using various means. There is a great deal of potential for distortion to the point where a scale ratio is meaningless. A small rule with indicated lengths drawn onto the plan will travel with the drawing and make measuring much easier on reproduced plans.

Topography

The shape of the land will influence access, supervision, aesthetics, aspect and drainage, to name but a few. It can also be used to create the feel of a space and provide inspiration for design features; for example, a slope might inspire a trickle stream, a terraced garden or an embedded slide. A professional site survey plan with contour lines preferably with 200 mm intervals or at least spot levels is essential to accurately design for effective drainage.

Existing structures

Any existing structures, for example buildings, pathways, fences and gates, shade and shelter, on the site need to be located and their dimensions and materials noted on the plan. Designing a playspace may also provide an opportunity to review the usefulness, positioning and soundness of existing structures and possibilities of relocation or reuse.

Significant plants

It is important to note not only the location of large trees, but also to give some indication of their crown and trunk diameter. Large established trees may be sensitive to major construction occurring within their root zone and the crown of a tree can be a good indication of an appropriate zone of exclusion for construction work. Whilst it is a good idea that all the trees on the site should have the dead wood removed prior to construction, commencing design is also the ideal time to ensure any potentially unhealthy trees are inspected by an arborist for possible removal. Developing a design that centres on a large tree which subsequently dies can leave a big hole in a play space.

Drainage and fall

Identify existing drains and pipes, but also establish where the site drains to naturally and where the water then goes. Water conservation is an increasing concern, so simply installing drainage that takes all the natural flow off site and into the storm water system can be counter productive to the ongoing viability of the site and be a missed opportunity for responsible re-use of a precious resource.

Prevailing winds

Winds can have a significant impact on site usage and children's behaviour, so consult with people who have a historical familiarity with the site over a long period of time to establish what wind problems exist on site. Significant planting, fencing or built structures such as storage areas may be strategically incorporated into the design to minimise prevailing wind effects.

Seasonal trouble spots

Some sites exhibit particular seasonal traits including hot dry spots in summer or cool wet spots in winter. Making a note of these anecdotal issues reminds the designer to consider this during the design process and incorporate design elements to alleviate the problem, perhaps turning a cool wet spot into a fernery for dinosaur play and a hot dry spot into an indigenous garden.

Surrounding land use

The surrounding land use has major implications for access, climate, safety and aesthetics. For example, busy roads and car parks need to be screened from view, neighbours may appreciate some privacy through planting, and views of adjoining parklands through a fence create a sense of never ending green space. Consultation with local stakeholders may reveal particular issues to be addressed in the design.

Consultation/reference groups

Community consultation is a critical element in making provision for a new outdoor playspace in an early childhood centre. This does not mean that the community should design the space, but does mean that they are given a reasonable opportunity to express their expectations and aspirations for the space. Consultation with the community is intended to establish desirable outcomes, concerns and wish lists. It is the task of the design consultant to facilitate the consultation and then match these with the other parameters associated with the playspace development.

Stakeholders in the community who have a direct impact on what is in an early childhood playspace can include licensing agents and advisors, government agencies, owners, staff, children and parents. Further to this, there are issues relating to Australian Standards, knowledge of equipment and materials, construction parameters and site conditions that need to be addressed during the consultation process.

In order to establish a community consultation process, the scope of the community to be engaged needs to be established. There is a myriad of groups associated with an early childhood centre and each needs to be involved at some level, including:

■ centre director/co-ordinator and staff;
■ licensing agent or organisational advisor;
■ parents;
■ children;
■ the wider community; and
■ the designer.

What would you like in your playspace?

A visual display is an excellent way to invite comment about the possibilities for the playspace and feedback on proposed plans.

Centre director/co-ordinator and staff

The director/co-ordinator and staff of the centre will have ideas and aspirations as to how the centre program is to be developed and implemented and what implications this has for the outdoor space. They will be able to offer significant local knowledge about the physical nature of the site (for example, prevailing winds, sunny hot-spots, supervision blind spots, storage access, drainage issues, and so on) that may not be apparent during the few visits a design consultant may make to the site. They also have significant knowledge of early childhood philosophy and practices that will impact on the playspace development (for example, indoor/outdoor programs, staff ratios, age appropriate playspaces). It will be up to the staff to utilise and manage the site once it is constructed, so their input is critical. Staff can gain a sense of participation in the planning and a belief that their expertise is appreciated as well as their needs understood through consultation.

Licensing agent or organisational advisor

It is best to engage personally with the licensing agent or organisational advisor early in the process, so that they can advise of concerns before the community become attracted to an element that may not be approved by relevant authorities. Also, contact with the local government responsible for the area will determine whether design approval is required and how the development may be viewed when it is submitted. The designer can perform this process, but it is often better for the centre director/co-ordinator to take this role as they can then develop an ongoing and sympathetic relationship with people whom they will have continuing contact.

Parents

Parental input is desirable as they have chosen to send their child to the centre, have particular aspirations for the playspace and may wish to contribute to the playspace development. Their contribution may range from fund raising cake stalls, or writing funding submissions, to hands-on planting or building. It is also critical to keep the parents informed as the process proceeds and to make clear to them how they can influence outcomes and provide feedback.

Children

Children—and facilitating their play—are central to the purpose of the project, so do not overlook the opportunity to engage with the children. Consultation with children is always revealing as children have their own perspective of space and place that adults can become distanced from. Children tend to view places and spaces in a more symbolic play value sense, rather than through the lens of physical practicalities that can dominate adult thinking. It is necessary to genuinely ascertain what children aspire to, rather than become lost in what adults think is good for children, and then provide a balance of both.

Children are entitled to input into how the space intended to challenge and engage them on a daily basis is developed. The language to elicit input must be chosen carefully. If you ask what they want in the playspace they may respond based on their local council playground comprised of coloured pipe and bark chip and answers may be unintentionally directed toward shopping lists of play equipment and little else. Whereas, if you ask them where their favourite places to play are or what they like to do in their playspace, a broader perception of the environment may be achieved. The use of visual representation —inviting them to draw or create with collage, clay or play dough, their ideal playspace—may offer alternatives to direct questioning. Visual representation challenges children to interpret space and identify elements that have significance and play meaning for them.

Wider community

The scale of community consultation will be proportional to the scale and intent of the proposed playspace development. This can range from a parent newsletter item to arranging facilitated public meetings from a diverse selection of individuals and special interest groups. Public meetings can also be everything from essentially unattended to crowded with significant debate.

A person with experience in facilitating, and one informed about the issues, is a valuable asset at meetings if the magnitude of the development or a prior knowledge of possible contentious issues warrants it. In order to manage the level of consultation, it may be necessary to establish conduits of information between the various interested parties—some projects establish reference groups. It may be that a new early childhood service has a reference group for the whole project with a sub group working on the outdoor playspace.

The reference group can comprise a variety of people, but generally have a fairly specific range of issues such as access, safety, environment and cost, that they wish to monitor. During the planning process, designated individuals from the reference group will monitor developments relating to their specific interest and then report their observations back to the reference group and larger community with the intention of generating collective feedback.

The designer

It is important to stress that consultation does not mean that any particular group does the actual design. The designer or consultant is often the only person who understands the broad range of influences from the community, the client, the interested groups and the specific site conditions. They may also be familiar with new opportunities for play not previously seen by the community as well as having an understanding of construction and plant materials. They also understand their responsibilities regarding the Australian Playground Standards and relevant state or local regulations.

Community consultation is critical to establishing the range of aspirations and expectations, previous usage and proposed intent but, ultimately, the designer must bring this all together into the broader parameters.

Concept design plans

Concept design plans or sketches need to establish a vision of how the site will be developed into a playspace. This must be done in a way that communicates the intended usage, proposed materials, indicative planting, finished surfaces, constructed elements and a sense of how the new development relates to the buildings and surrounding land use including possible implications for parking, noise and infrastructure.

All this must be done in a manner that makes the drawings accessible to people not familiar with reading plans. The scale of the drawing is critical as some scales do not allow sufficient detail to appropriately inform those reading them.

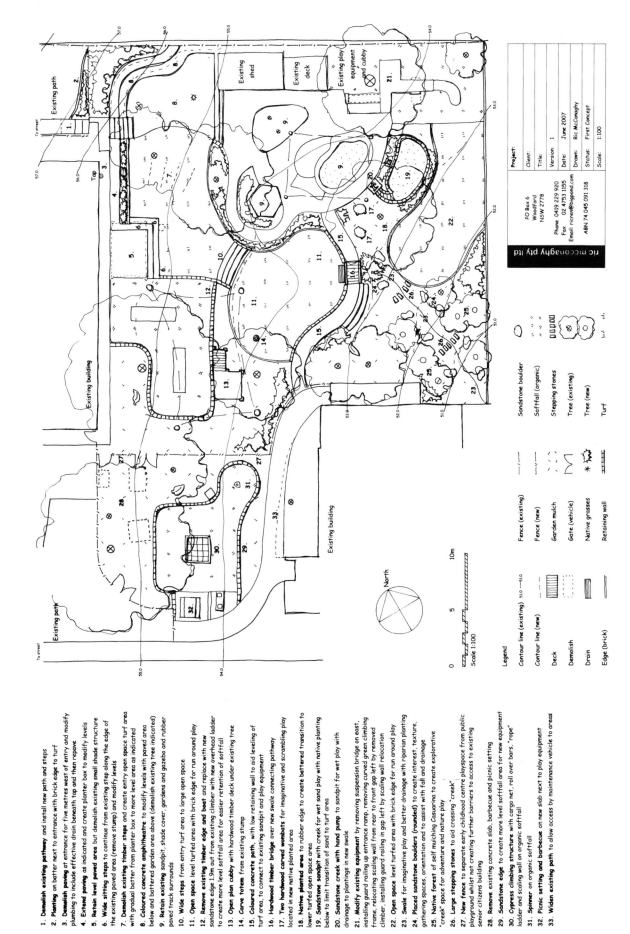

1. **Demolish existing pathway** and install new path and steps
2. **Planting** on batter next to entrance with brick edge to turf
3. **Demolish paving** at entrance for five metres west of entry and modify plumbing to include effective drain beneath tap and then repave
4. **Extend paving** as indicated and create planter box to modify levels
5. **Retain level paved area** but demolish existing small shade structure
6. **Wide sitting steps** to continue from existing step along the edge of the existing paved area (remove stump) and modify levels
7. **Demolish existing timber steps** and create entry open space turf area with gradual batter from planter box to more level area as indicated
8. **Coloured concrete amphitheatre** to modify levels with paved area below and battered garden area above (demolish existing tree indicated)
9. **Retain existing sandpit**, shade cover, gardens and gazebo and rubber paved track surrounds
10. **Wide steps** from entry turf area to large open space
11. **Open space level** turfed area with brick edge for run around play
12. **Remove existing timber edge and boat** and replace with new sandstone edge 1.9m out from existing climber with new overhead ladder to create more level soffall area for easier retention of soffall
13. **Open plan cubby** with hardwood timber deck under existing tree
14. **Carve totem** from existing stump
15. **Coloured concrete path**, with low retaining wall to aid leveling of turf area, to connect to existing sandpit and play equipment
16. **Hardwood timber bridge** over new swale connecting pathway
17. **Two hardwood carved wombats** for imaginative and scrambling play located in new native planted area
18. **Native planted area** to rubber edge to create battered transition to lower turfed open space area
19. **Sandstone sandpit** with creek for wet sand play with native planting below to limit transition of sand to turf area
20. **Sandstone creek with hand pump** to sandpit for wet play with drainage to plantings in new swale
21. **Modify existing equipment** by removing suspension bridge on east, installing guard railing up entrance ramp, removing curved green climbing frame, relocating scaling wall from rear to front gap left by removed climber, installing guard railing in gap left by scaling wall relocation
22. **Open space level** turfed area with brick edge for run around play
23. **Swale** for imaginative play and better drainage with riparian planting
24. **Placed sandstone boulders** (rounded) to create interest, texture, gathering spaces, orientation and to assist with fall and drainage
25. **Native forest** of self mulching Casuarina to create explorative "creek" space for adventure and nature play
26. **Large stepping stones** to aid crossing "creek"
27. **New fence** to separate early childhood centre playspace from public playground whilst not creating further barriers to access to existing senior citizens building
28. **Remove existing concrete slab**, barbecue and picnic setting
29. **Sandstone edge** to create more level soffall area for new equipment
30. **Cypress climbing structure** with cargo net, roll over bars, "rope" ladder and scaling wall on organic soffall
31. **Spinner** on organic soffall
32. **Picnic setting and barbecue** on new slab next to play equipment
33. **Widen existing path** to allow access by maintenance vehicle to areas

An example of an outdoor playspace concept design plan for an early childhood centre.

Legend

Contour line (existing) 51.0 —— 51.0	Sandstone boulder
Contour line (new)	Soffall (organic)
Deck	Stepping stones
Demolish	Tree (existing)
Drain	Tree (new)
Edge (brick)	Turf
Fence (existing)	
Fence (new)	
Garden mulch	
Gate (vehicle)	
Native grasses	
Retaining wall	

North

Scale 1:100
0   5   10m

ric mcconaghy pty ltd

PO Box 6
Woodford
NSW 2778

Phone 0419 229 920
Fax   02 4753 1155
Email: ricren@bigpond.com

ABN 74 045 091 318

Project:	
Client:	
Title:	
Version:	1
Date:	June 2007
Drawn:	Ric McConaghy
Status:	First Concept
Scale:	1:100

The scale of 1:100 for site drawings gives a good impression of space allocation and the relationship of one centimetre representing one metre is relatively easy to apply with a standard measure ruler. It is critical to indicate orientation, so that the implications of seasonal influence on the site can be considered. A legend describing all the different surfaces and installations is essential. In addition, a scaled site model may be a useful tool to visualise the playspace and, particularly, to invite comment from children.

Feedback/review/design development

There is a multitude of ways for the designer to obtain feedback on the proposed design plan. Having already undertaken community consultation, those people previously contacted can be involved in a review and feedback process. The centre could arrange an evening in which the centre staff, the community, interested groups and parents are invited to 'walk through' the plan by the designer. Indicative photographs and illustrations can be useful for clarification during the review process, particularly if the feedback process is simply a notice board display inviting comment. The designer has a significant role to interpret and analyse the collated feedback, then review and redesign as required. A further round of feedback and review of the revised plans is important to ensure the final plan meets the expectations and aspirations of the centre community.

Opinion of probable cost

Even with the desire of the community to provide an inviting natural outdoor playspace for children there are always financial parameters attached to any construction project. It is best to try and present the opinion of probable cost schedules on a task by task basis so that communities can determine the value added on any proposed element. For communities who intend to do much of their own work, it is still sensible to determine a commercial value for all the work and use this as one of the criterion for decision-making about what tasks might be completed by volunteers. The type of task and skills of volunteers also need to be considered in the community decision-making process. No matter how much free labour or skills are available, there will still be costs associated with each task such as hiring machinery and purchasing materials or plants, so an opinion of probable cost is useful.

Staging plan

Sometimes projects will need to be staged. A priority of need applied to a thorough understanding of site implications for any present or future development should be explored before final decisions on staging are made. For example, drainage would be a priority of need over ground surfacing while other needs could be addressed in tandem, such as installation of a rainwater tank and digging patch. Staging may also involve identifying volunteer work that can be undertaken by the local community to support the development, consideration of peak centre usage times and seasonal changes.

Final concept design

Having engaged in the process of design and review, a final concept plan must be prepared. This is the document that is a sign-off record of what the community aspires to. This document will then be the basis for the preparation of construction documentation for tendering purposes.

Approvals

Before proceeding to tender it is essential to confirm if any agencies need to approve the proposed developments. All early childhood centres in Australia need to confirm with their licensing agents in each state that their proposed development conforms with the licensing regulations and requirements. Agencies that will have an interest include relevant state and local government departments. State and local governments throughout Australia have differing requirements for approval so it is essential to make contact and seek advice.

Tender documentation

As the concept plan must communicate to the community at large the intention of the design, so the tender documentation should provide the landscape contractor with as much information as possible in order to accurately price and then successfully tender for and construct the vision. The construction drawing should be accompanied by a Specification document so that the contractor understands the nature of the construction and the quality of finish expected. The Specification document describes in detail all the elements of the design including the types of materials to be used and specific information about construction of design features to support the construction drawing. It should also advise the landscape contractor of their responsibilities regarding relevant standards, timing, establishment, clean up and maintenance. A Bill of Quantities (or Schedule of Rates) listing the quantities of materials to be used should be attached to the Specification document to facilitate cost comparison. A rates column should be included in the Bill of Quantities, so that if variations occur during construction the client will be informed as to the revised rate per volume of material applicable.

Tendering/contractor selection

Having taken the time and care to determine the appropriate designer/ consultant, engaged in a thorough and inclusive consultation process and determined the optimum design for the site, the choice of contractor to construct the space is crucial. The contractor will be the ultimate conduit for the success of the project. The tender can be an open process or the documents can be sent to a number of selected tenderers who have relevant experience. It is advisable to send the documents to at least five contractors/organisations. Usually at least three quotes are desired and sending out at least five requests to tender ensures this target is reached. Of course, the more tender submissions, the better it is to compare prices and achieve a positive outcome.

When checking tender submissions and selecting a contractor, it is critical to be aware that the cheapest may not be the best. In addition to the actual tender submission, contractor interviews can be very revealing in determining whether a contractor really understands the nature of the project and the outcome desired. The tendering contractor must have seen the site and be aware that the space is intended for intensive use by children for most of the year. This will require robust construction as well as very specific attention to detail in finishes, particularly edges and transitional points. Some contractors specialise in children's playspaces and understand these aspects, whereas others may just try to build it as quickly and cheaply as possible. Individual parents may be in a hurry to get the space built before their child leaves the centre and may naturally seek the lowest price. But, the space will be a legacy left for some time and will continue to evolve, so it is critical the foundation laid can support ongoing development.

It is recommended that the people assessing the tender submissions visit sites that the tenderers have constructed to assess the quality of work and talk to previous clients. The tenderer should provide a portfolio of completed projects and a list of referees that can be contacted.

The type of contract between the client and the contractor will vary substantially depending on the scale of the project. The contract is intended to protect all parties and to ensure processes are in place for resolution of any issues during construction. Large corporations generally supply their own contracts which should be thoroughly read before signing. It is advisable that independent legal advice be sought if any aspects need clarification. An alternative, if no contract is supplied, is to use one of the standard contracts available. Seek advice from Standards Australia or a legal practitioner as to the most appropriate one for your needs.

Construction administration

In order that the construction proceeds in an appropriate and timely manner, some centres choose to engage a third party to perform contract administration. This is done because those in early childhood education rarely have expertise in construction and may not be able to ensure the tasks are being performed appropriately according to the construction drawings and design plan. The role of this person is to ensure the intent of the design is maintained and to be a conduit for communication between the parties involved.

Holistic view of the playspace as a naturalistic environment

In closing we should consider how we want our children to perceive the world. Vast expanses of rubber softfall, structured equipment and highly engineered shade structures offer a very artificial and fairly rigid example of the world, particularly for someone attending the same playspace five days a week for a year or more.

That is not to say that these things should be excluded, but that we should endeavour to provide a balance of built form and natural form. Many children will have preference for certain experiences and will drift toward them most days, but by offering balance we allow for those days when they desire something different.

If your particular reference group remains unconvinced about the advantages of natural spaces then the final fallback position is money! For example, the amount of money spent on shade structures will nearly always be more than that required to purchase and plant well advanced trees. Further, trees become an appreciating asset rather than a depreciating one and with deciduous trees there are the advantages of shade in summer, but sun in winter and loose parts for play. Similarly, installing slides on mounds and other appropriate equipment at less than 500 mm above the ground not only encourages more children to engage, but also saves outlay on vast softfall areas if designed properly. Many early childhood centres have limited financial resources, but have still managed to create places of wonder, intrigue and challenge with relatively low budgets. At the very least it is worth doing the sums.

References

Berry P, 2001, *Playgrounds that Work. Creating Outdoor Play Environments For Children Birth to Eight Years*, Pademelon Press, Sydney.

Greenman J, 1996, *Caring Spaces, Learning Places: Children's Environments that Work*, Exchange Press, USA.

Kirkby M, 1989, 'Nature as Refuge in Children's Environments', *Children's Environments Quarterly*, Vol 6 No 1, Spring pp 7–12.

KU Children's Services, 2004, *KU Environment Policy*, KU Children's Services, Sydney.

Website resources

Australian Institute of Landscape Architects
www.aila.org.au/

Australian Institute of Landscape Designers and Managers
www.aildm.com.au/

Building Code of Australia
www.wst.tas.gov.au/resource/bsrbuildingc.htm

Landscape Contractors Association of New South Wales
www.lcansw.com.au/

Standards Australia
www.standards.com.au/

Creating specific
features to foster nature
connections

Tracy Young

3

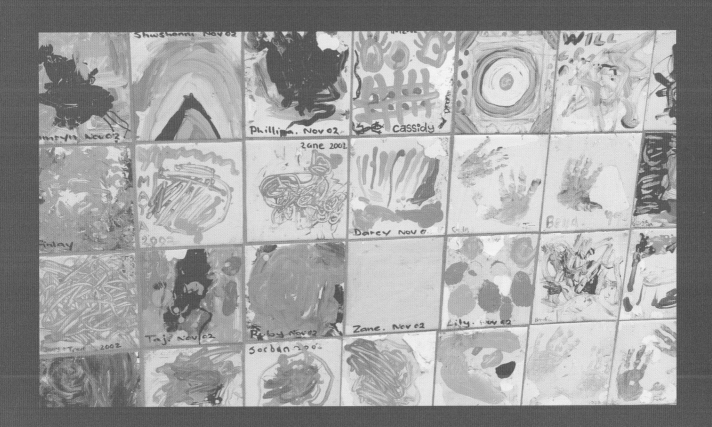

Introduction

If we ask each other what we value in life, family is often top of the list. We love our family, care for family members and would do anything to protect them. Do we feel this same connection to nature? Many indigenous peoples throughout history have felt this same connection with the natural world. It was a connection that enabled them to live from the land using sustainable practices for thousands of years. Perhaps we can learn some lessons from these belief systems and practices?

Nearly 150 years ago, Chief Seattle, a leader of one of the Native American Nations, delivered a compelling message to the American Government who wanted to buy his land. He believed that all life on earth, and the earth itself, is sacred, and that human beings heedless abuse of nature will lead to their destruction (Chief Seattle quoted in Jeffers, 1991):

> 'This we know' All things are connected like the blood that unites us. We did not weave the web of life, we are merely a stand in it. Whatever we do to the web, we do to ourselves.

How do young children perceive the natural world? For that matter, how do educators who work with children perceive the natural world? Is the natural world a part of who we are as people? A part of our everyday lives? Or is the natural world something that is 'out there' to be enjoyed or feared at certain times or used for our very survival? The answer to these questions varies from person to person, place to place, and over time. However, increasingly, human beings in the twenty-first century have become more removed from the natural world. Within western culture, we now define 'nature' and 'wild' in a more distanced, abstract way—a way that is external to ourselves, not a part of who we are. This disconnection can be witnessed in the outdoor playspaces we provide for children.

Louv (2005) makes the case that today's children are more alienated from the natural world than ever before. Children may be aware of the global threats to the environment, but their physical contact, their intimacy with nature, is fading. 'When children do interact with nature ... they are more likely to do so through organized activities than through the kind of casual exploring that once defined childhood. Children don't "discover" nature now; they are "shown" it, often on guided trips through the woods' (Louv, 2005, p 12). Or, children experience nature vicariously through looking at beautiful glossy photographs in books or watching films or nature documentaries on television.

The following two examples reflect current perceptions of the natural world held by adults and children:

1. An Australian study examined sixth grade children's concepts of nature and children's responses to questions often indicated that they saw nature as something external to humans. One child, when asked if nature is also a koala in a zoo, stated that koalas have been harmed by humans so were no longer natural (Payne, 1998, p 21). This was a common response from primary school aged children in this study who perceived nature as being 'something that has not been touched or harmed by humans'.

2. The second example comes from a participant in a workshop entitled 'Connecting young children with the natural world'. The participant was a very enthusiastic teacher who described an activity planned for some young children who were interested in snails. She painted a number on

each of the snails' shells with correction fluid and then placed them on a piece of black cardboard to race and see who would be the winner. Why would this teacher feel that this was helping children connect with nature? Is it natural for snails to race; is it not enough to examine the silvery trails left on the cardboard? Is it harmful to a snail to have a toxic chemical placed on its shell and more importantly what message is conveyed to children about living creatures?

Perceiving nature as an internal rather than an external component helps to demonstrate a view of the natural world as a part of the human experience, something worth protecting. An exploration of the four elements—humans, the land, plants and animals—and their inter-relatedness is vital to feeling connected to the natural world. It is also a difficult concept for children to grasp and can be overlooked by educators. If humans feel separated from nature they are less likely to appreciate, respect and therefore care for the natural systems that sustain us. Playspace design features that include a human element will help to foster this connection and ensure that nature is not a separate entity that only occasionally touches our lives.

'As a scientist I have come to know that … We are made up of water, air and the food we eat from the Earth's soil. I've come to realise ... it is a mistake to think of the environment as something "out there", separate from us. We are the Earth…' (Suzuki and Vanderlinden, 1999, p 6).

This chapter provides a wealth of ideas for the inclusion of specific natural design features in early childhood outdoor playspaces, for both the novice and more experienced educators/naturalists. The focus is on inspirations rather than duplications, as designs should adapt to meet the sociocultural needs of each centre and the communities they are located within. For more specific landscape or architecture design features, the reader should consult specialist references, landscape architects or landscape design companies. The intention here is to prompt the reader to consider the importance of natural elements within the outdoor playspace. Whether this manifests as quick and easy changes, such as large logs or boulders, or a full scale building project, like a watercourse, will depend on budget, motivation and the philosophy of the centre. Some centres may desire to change an artificial outdoor playspace to a more natural playspace, while other centres may already incorporate many elements from nature, with a desire to include more, or add sustainable practices into the program.

An interesting observation from the many beautiful natural outdoor spaces I visited in preparation for this chapter, is that the staff and families have generally not relied on experts or local councils to create the playspaces. This is not to say that professional advice is not worthwhile, but budgets do not always stretch to using professionals. Centres that create their own natural playspaces often display a strong sense of connectedness and ownership that prompts further improvement. The inherent message is perhaps to 'just do it', grow some plants, design a play feature, collect some natural materials or visit inspirational centres for further ideas.

The role of professional services and a clear planning process should not however be overlooked. 'Regrettably the planning and designing of early childhood centre playgrounds is not given the priority that an area of such constant daily usage and importance deserves' (Walsh, 1991, p 9). Successful playspaces are designed with knowledge of child development, safety standards, play and the natural environment. Educators, designers and landscape architects need to work together to provide the optimum natural playspace. The Ian Potter Foundation Children's Garden at the Royal Botanic Gardens Melbourne is a perfect example of this multidisciplinary approach. Staff from the Royal Botanic Gardens embarked upon wide consultation with child education groups, travelled to observe other children's gardens throughout the world and researched children's play. The result is a stunning garden with unique features that combine educational and horticultural expertise. The Gardens encourage great freedom, elements of risk and active exploration as children run through the flax tunnel, crawl into the fossilised hollow tree, explore the changing land formations and experience the wildlife in the large lake. Such wild, natural areas are often missing from children's lives. Nabhan and Trimble (1994) explore this notion of wild places and discover interesting research about children's intrinsic need to create cubbies and concealed areas, removed from adults. How can we balance the need for safety and supervision, but still ensure children's play needs are met? How can we ensure that children still have places to tunnel, dig, climb and experience lush vegetation and a sense of wildness? The children and families of Melbourne and Victoria owe a debt of gratitude to The Royal Botanic Gardens for developing an inspiring and appropriate children's garden. I only hope the children of the future will not have to visit these gardens to experience nature in the way they visit a zoo to experience wild animals. Children need nature in their lives every day.

This is a native bottle tree, named because of the bottle-shaped trunk that stores water and is therefore part of the succulent family of plants. Bottle trees are native to Queensland, but will grow in many other parts of Australia. These trees surround embedded water spouts at the entrance to The Ian Potter Foundation Children's Garden at the Royal Botanic Gardens in Melbourne. The trees are just the right scale for young children to huddle under!

Specific design features

If we were to ask young children what they enjoyed outdoors or observe the kind of outdoor spaces that interest and sustain their play, we would probably identify the manipulatory and loose materials such as mud, water, sand, rocks, seed pods, leaves and logs as essential. They would enjoy discovering snails or ants in leaf litter, the pleasure of eating a strawberry grown in the garden, the challenge of climbing a tree or hiding in cool thick shrubbery on a summer's day. They would enjoy the company of peers and an adult who can help them discover more about the world they live in and foster a sense of wonder. These are the elements children might enjoy; the challenge for playspace designers is to create features that afford such pleasures.

A well-designed outdoor playspace for young children also ensures there are opportunities for many levels of play and activity. Children need places to sit, manipulate, create, jump, run, build, climb, imagine, discover and wonder. The design needs to consider quiet and active areas and reflect the age and number of children and adults who use the space. A number of specific design features such as places of interest, aesthetic elements, animals, natural elements and plants can be incorporated to afford pleasure and meet the diverse and dynamic needs of young children.

Places of interest

Places of interest may provide foci for planning, a destination, an invitation to play or promote functionality of the outdoor space. In the following paragraphs, wild places, cubbies, secret places, verandahs and pergolas, wooden platforms and amphitheatres, mounds, paths and arches will be considered as places of interest.

Wild places

Children enjoy wild places with lush plantings and opportunities for calculated risk. Nabhan and Trimble (1994) identify children's intrinsic need for such places—concealed spaces with 'nest-like' vegetation that is away from adult eyes. Adult visions of children's playspaces often reflect the local park with fixed swings, slides and seesaws. These may be fun places to visit for short periods of time, but children may not enjoy spending lengthy periods of time at the park. According to child psychologist Sutton-Smith (cited in Nabhan and Trimble, 1994) playspaces have become increasingly barren with less enclosed or wild areas. 'To counter the historic trend toward the loss of wildness where children play, it is clear that we need to find ways to let children roam beyond the pavement, to gain access to vegetation and earth that allows them to tunnel, climb or even fall … I would like to see kids have more smells, tastes, splinters and accidents' (Nabhan and Trimble, 1994, p 9).

This tree has not had the lower limbs pruned so children can climb the branches easily to lookout points. The beauty of nature is also evident in this tranquil green playspace of the Melbourne Rudolph Steiner School.

Flax is a hardy plant that can be used to create wild places. This flax tunnel has hundreds of children running through it weekly at The Ian Potter Foundation Children's Garden at the Royal Botanic Gardens Melbourne.

This cubby at Bairnsdale Early Learning Centre has been made with two rose arbours secured into the ground. A flowering passionfruit vine grew quickly to provide a natural plant cover. Soft items like carpets, blankets and cushions are a welcome addition, creating cosy home-like spaces.

Cubbies

Young children enjoy exploring nooks and crannies; this is evident when children hide behind a shed or crawl into small spaces. Children seem to have an innate need for child-sized spaces, which offer privacy and social intimacy outdoors and the play is often different to the play observed in larger, open active areas. Cubbies give children a sense of belonging; they offer emotional security and comfort and promote child initiated pretend play. Provide secluded areas for cubbies hidden from adults, but still in view to ensure adequate supervision. Older children can construct bush cubbies from natural resources such as branches or fronds or, alternatively, trees provide stable points to attach fabric for tent-like cubbies that work particularly well with infants and toddlers. The found loose parts in a natural playspace such as leaves, tan bark and pods then facilitate pretend play in the cubby.

Haybales have been used to make a cubby for dramatic play at St Kilda and Balaclava Kindergarten. The hay was later used on the garden beds when it started to decompose.

Plantings of Lomandra create this quiet, hidden area at The University of Melbourne Early Learning Centre Abbotsford.

Secret places

Secret places are quiet areas that enable children to retreat from active areas in the playspace. It may be useful to plan these for small groups or even solitary play opportunities. Children enjoy moments of contemplation and the inclusion of plant materials encourages backyard creatures such as butterflies, ants and snails to the space. In addition to plants, timber lattice and bamboo, wicker or brush screens can help to create secret spaces.

This experience is located in the hidden garden it is designed for one child and or a quiet place for an adult and child to share a book at Shelford Early Learning Centre.

This centre has created many divided areas in the outside playspace including a hidden garden where children can get away from the main group at Shelford Early Learning Centre.

This fossilised tree creates a place for investigation and discovery at the Royal Botanic Gardens Ian Potter Foundation Children's Garden.

This service has chosen to incorporate large wooden deck areas with verandahs, so children can use the space in hot or wet weather. The space also lends itself to an indoor/outdoor program with the large doors that lead outside. The children at Monash Children's Centre Beddoe Avenue like to watch the rain from this space. Note the importance of colour in this setting.

Verandahs and pergolas

Verandahs and covered pergola areas provide useful shade and protection from the natural elements. They enable outside spaces to be used all year in hot, windy or wet weather. They are also useful for the temporary storage of equipment at the end of the day. Verandahs and pergolas need to be considered in the overall architectural design of the building and planned to facilitate a positive and workable relationship between indoor and outdoor spaces.

Wooden platforms and amphitheatres

Using natural materials such as wood enhances the aesthetic appeal of a playspace. Wood adds warmth and can be oiled to maintain the surface and highlight the natural grain of the wood. Hardwoods or treated softwoods are required for outside use. It would be beneficial to source sustainable timbers such as plantation softwood or recycled hardwood timbers.

Wooden platforms enable children to view the world from a different height; they also add different perspectives to the playspace to minimise the flat, bland panoramic view. Good design principles incorporate differing levels to provide interest and aesthetic appeal. Platforms may require guardrails to prevent fall injures. Always check with state children's services regulations and Standards Australia (refer to Chapter 5).

Outdoor amphitheatres can be used for dramatic play, plays, dress-ups, music, puppets or any activities that require a defined space. The raised platform provides a stage for play and the addition of seating provides a vantage point to watch the play or an ideal space for discussion, stories and outdoor mealtimes.

Copper Chrome Arsenate (CCA) is used to treat timber against pest infestation and rotting. From March 2006, as a precautionary measure, the Australian Pesticides and Veterinary Medicines Authority (APVMA) recommended that CCA treated timber no longer be permitted in some applications and structures including the building of new garden furniture, picnic tables, exterior seating, children's play equipment, patios, domestic decking and handrails. The APVMA has not recommended the removal of existing structures. There is no reason to remove or replace CCA-treated structures that are in good condition. This includes playground equipment. There are arsenic-free alternative timber treatment products that are registered for use in Australia and these products control a similar range of pests. Ask your timber supplier or hardware store about alternatives that are suitable. Also, consult your local state government, Kidsafe NSW or PRAV for up to date information about CCA treated timber.

These platforms create an interesting playspace surrounded by an indigenous garden at St Leonard's Cornish Campus.

This amphitheatre is shaded by the large tree and provides endless opportunities for open-ended play at The University of Melbourne Early Learning Centre Abbotsford.

Mounds

Mounds provide variations of ground surfaces that create interest and reflect the natural landscape. Many playspaces are flat so a mound can be a valuable inclusion. Even a one metre mound can be challenging for toddlers and pre-school aged children for climbing, running, rolling down and sitting on. If the mound is covered in grass the slope ratio needs to be no greater than 1:3; this means for every metre in height there needs to be 3 metres of width around the mound. This slope ratio prevents erosion and enables easy mowing (Corkery, 1987, p 46).

These grassy mounds provide just the right challenge for active toddlers at The Ian Potter Foundation Children's Garden at the Royal Botanic Gardens Melbourne.

Paths and arches

Pathways help provide defined links between different areas. Paths need to be wide enough for wheel chairs and wheeled play props such as prams and wheelbarrows. Mosaic tiles, gravel, stones, granitic sand or tree stump stepping-stones can all be used to create pathways. Arches and bridges are also useful ways to link defined spaces together and create a sense of surprise and wonder. Where do the pathways lead? What is hidden beyond the arches?

These natural plant archways at Coombes Infant School divide the playspace like a room in a house creating intimate areas that change the focus of children's play. They are also a real invitation to explore!

An inexpensive timber bridge like this one creates a varied landscape at Monash Children's Centre Beddoe Avenue.

Aesthetic elements—The human factor

The colours, senses and elements of nature

Television makeover shows could lead one to believe that children's playspaces should be brightly coloured with a dominance of primary colours. Whilst there may be some evidence that young infants respond to bright colours, bright colours assault the senses rather than create aesthetically pleasing environments. Nature provides a wealth of beauty and coloured hues that do not dominate the senses. Flowers, varied textures, enticing scents and shades of green have a particularly soothing effect. The natural playspace can mirror the beauty of nature.

This sensory garden at Keysborough Community Children's Centre comprised of herbs, flowers and strawberries began in tyres. As the plants grew the staff designed a waist high garden bed where the sensory plants are now at children's level encouraging them to smell and touch the plants. One of the favourites with the children is the herb that smells like curry.

This seated area is often used by parents at Monash Children's Centre Beddoe Avenue as they collect children at the end of a busy day.

Other suitable plants for a sensory garden include:

- plants with textured leaves such as lambs ear (*Stachys byzantia*);
- succulents that have interesting leaf formations;
- brightly coloured flowering annuals or perennials;
- herbs that smell or can be eaten including parsley, rosemary, thyme, sage, lemon balm, mint and coriander; and
- native grasses or casuarina trees that move gently in the wind creating a rustling sound.

Physical needs and a sense of wellbeing

Timber seats should be located in quiet areas and this area may have a number of uses as a place:

- for quietly exploring a book;
- to be alone or with a friend;
- to sit in the shade of the tree or be sheltered from the wind;
- for staff to sit strategically located to supervise children; and
- for parents and staff to sit comfortably and feel this is a place for them to enjoy too.

Wattletree Early Learning Centre has a combined toddler and pre-school playspace with many natural features. The harmony garden is a space for quiet contemplation. Note the birdhouse in the background.

Incorporating art into the playspace

Human beings are greatly affected by artwork and playspaces that include art increase the aesthetic appeal of the outdoor environment and invite adults and children to enjoy and explore the environment. Artwork is a way to include the human element into the natural playspace and emphasise the connection between humans, plants, animals and the land. Many of the materials used to create art have natural origins such as clay, stone, ochre, paints, fabric and plant fibres or seedpods. Children benefit from visual art in the playspace, particularly if local artists are invited to share their work and skills with children.

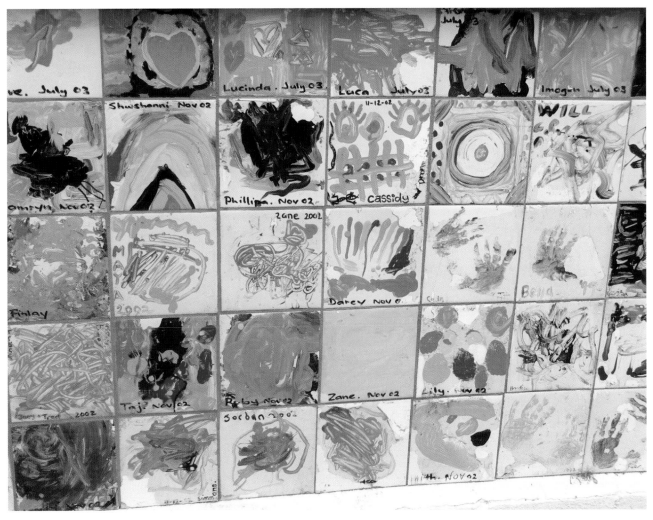

These tiles were painted by all the children linked to Tennyson Street Children's Centre providing a record of their presence. The tiles were mounted onto a wall near the entrance.

Australian Indigenous art links nature, family and community themes. This mural incorporates Indigenous art into the children's playspace at Audrey Brooks Memorial Pre School.

'Our kindergarten is on Wurundjeri land. Inside our gate is a painting. It's an Aboriginal painting. The Wurundjeri people are Aboriginal—Indigenous people. Our painting tells a story. Inside the gate is a waterhole. Next to the fence is a lizard and some possum tracks. Next to the garden is a turtle. The animals meet at the waterhole for a yarn. There are some kids' footprints leaving the waterhole and some emu tracks. A long, long snake is past the footprints. Next to the door is a campfire and people sitting around it.'

Creating Specific Features to Foster Nature Connections

< 55 >

Sculptures and mosaics can be used effectively in the natural playspace and may reflect the local culture, history or landscape.

This sculpture (above) was commissioned after the tragic death of a much loved staff member at May Armstrong Child Care Centre. The staff and management committee commissioned Kevin Free to produce a sculpture for the preschool garden. The artwork is a memorial to Kellie, a staff colleague. It is a place for staff and children to visit and to find some comfort and peace in dealing with their loss of a loved friend.

The University of Melbourne Early Learning Centre Abbotsford includes numerous artworks—some (right and above right) for the aesthetic appeal and others that have been made with the children. The mosaic bowl was made by the children who were inspired by an ongoing project on stick insects that they explored through the year. Stick insects are very worthwhile and easily maintained classroom animals to study and investigate.

Animal care and discovery

The values that I and so many others learned from animals are perhaps some of the most significant lessons that a child can learn. They are so often passed on to children from a passionate adult who helps to open a child's senses to the wonder of nature. To watch the birth, or experience the death of a pet helps to prepare us for life (Young in Young and Elliott, 2003, p 16).

Children have a natural affinity to and curiosity about animals. Early childhood educators know that animals feature highly in children's interests yet early childhood centres are moving away from including live animals in the program. Meaningful opportunities for learning are promoted when caring for domestic animals or wild, native animals, on a long-term basis. Projects and everyday practices such as observation, cleaning and feeding, enable children to construct knowledge about animal biology, biodiversity, habitats, food, life cycles and the interconnectedness between plants, people, animals and the land. This knowledge and experience with animals is powerful, and the ultimate aim is to not only understand the connections with the natural world, but also encourage active citizens who speak out against cruelty. 'Voiceless', an Australian animal advocacy group states that 'Education is a powerful and effective means to foster the values of compassion and respect for animals in the younger generation. Animal education, often referred to as "humane educa-tion", is a growing field in many countries.' Animals can play a key role in the natural playspace where children can be exposed to attitudes of compassion and empathy and discover an appreciation for and connection with animals.

First-hand experience with animals can also help to allay fears or negative attitudes that children may have. This is difficult if adults also express fear or dislike for animals or resent the additional workload that animals create. Children quickly pick up on these negative emotions and a committed team of educators is needed to successfully include animals in the program. The lone 'animal lover' may struggle unless they have support from the team, so it may be easier to err on the side of caution and only include animals after reflecting on the team values. Animal welfare and hygiene are key considerations and children need to adhere to hand washing practices.

Native animals

Native animals may include animals that appear unexpectedly in the play-space or those that are kept in enclosures. In Australia these may include birds, blue tongue or other lizards, possums or minibeasts such as ants, stick insects, caterpillars or worms.

Frogs
A frog pond established to attract local frogs could become the focus of many learning opportunities about frog habitats and biodiversity. The life cycles of frogs provide clear examples of metamorphosis and a pond enables children to witness these changes up close. Do not collect frog's eggs, tadpoles or frogs from the wild: this is a common, but illegal practice. Seek advice from the relevant government department.

Blue tongue lizards
Blue tongue lizards are reptiles found in most parts of Australia. There are six types in Australia and they eat snails, slugs, flowers and fruit. Blue tongues can live for up to 30 years, are easy to care for and hibernate in cooler climates. They need a low, fenced enclosure that children cannot poke sticks into. Children

St Leonards Cornish Campus is lucky enough to have a river running through the grounds. This area of the river has been planted with reeds that attract frogs.

This naturalistic enclosure has been dug in a pit in the ground and surrounded with paving tiles. The lizards have water access and rocks and logs to hibernate under. This design enables children to actively observe, feed and study these blue tongued lizards. The children are aware of the life cycle and the need for the lizards to hibernate during a cold Melbourne winter.

These boxes become homes to birds and enable children to observe the breeding cycle of birds at St Leonards Cornish Campus.

are curious about animals and may not always treat them with respect. Clear Perspex provides good vision, but a more naturalistic enclosure may blend more easily into the playspace.

Native birds and bees

Birds create enormous potential for animal observation. Wild birds bring the delightful sensory element of sound to the playspace and a keen bird observer will be able to identify a bird by its call or birdsong. Attracting birds and native bees can be achieved by situating a range of timber habitat boxes outside. Seek information from experts in your area to source suitable boxes for your indigenous species. Bird baths and bird feeding trays can also be used to attract birds, however check with local wildlife groups to ensure that local birds do not become reliant on food you provide.

Native stingless bees are found in all states in Australia and provide interesting exploration of life cycles, pollination of native plants and honey production. Campus Kindy, University of Queensland, has established native hives in very small boxes that are easily managed. Native bees are small and have interesting social behaviour like the commercial honeybees, but they are stingless and easier to handle. The brood comb, containing the eggs, is often formed in a beautiful spiral and it is possible to extract a little bush honey from the clusters of honey pots. Native bees require specialist indigenous plants to feed from and the Australian native bee centre has a free Ebook outlining all the care requirements.

These native bees are considerably smaller than European bees and do not sting (Campus Kindy, University of Queensland).

Domestic animals

In the past, domestic animals have been common fixtures in early childhood centres; however, it is now rare to find chickens, rabbits or guinea pigs. Many children have a domesticated animal such as guinea pig or a rabbit as a first pet. These pets make excellent companions, but they are quite dependent on their owners to provide them with care and attention every day. Owning a pet provides a child with companionship and encourages the child's understanding of responsibility and care for dependent creatures. Children need to be actively involved with the care of animals. Adults, however, must at all times guide children in their handling of domesticated animals and be prepared to supervise the day-to-day care so that the animal is not neglected through ignorance or loss of interest. Also, remember there is not much point leaving a solitary animal in a cage where children do not feed, touch or investigate the animal. What message does this send to young children?

Furthermore, there is a tendency to view animals as a learning tool for children like a computer or book that they can glean knowledge from. This approach will not necessarily develop connections with the natural world and animals can be viewed as objects for human entertainment or knowledge. To foster authentic connections with animals, children need to experience ongoing caring relationships based on respect and compassion, where animals are seen as unique, feeling beings in their own right.

Information can be sourced from the RSPCA, local pet stores and specific animal interest groups about housing, breeding, care and characteristics of many domestic animals. Enclosures can be fixed features as illustrated below or wheelable/moveable if the playspace design is more suited to this option. Also, be mindful that some children may have feather or fur allergies and this may determine the type of animal kept at the centre.

Chickens

One never forgets the expression of a young child watching in amazement as a chicken hatches from an egg. Chicken life cycles are fascinating and create opportunities for children to be actively involved as they incubate eggs, care for the chicks, feed adult birds and collect eggs for cooking. Chickens can free range in the playspace where they become quite tame and feed on snails, small garden animals and plants. Children need to be reminded about respecting the chickens and not chasing them. Chickens need to be locked away in a fox-proof enclosure at night and weekends.

This chicken coop has been attached between a shed and the main building utilising a very simple design at Yooralla Pre School.

Guinea pigs (Cavies)

One of the most popular pet rodents, these are generally hardy animals and given a sheltered hutch outdoors they are easy to care for. Guinea pigs are docile with people and soon become tame and tractable with careful handling. Their size and shape allow them to be easily handled by children, preferably when children are seated. They are social animals, so it is necessary to keep more than one guinea pig for companionship.

Rabbits

Tame rabbits make attractive, appealing pets and are relatively hardy animals. Children can easily handle the smaller breeds of rabbit. Like guinea pigs, rabbits are social animals and require companionship of another rabbit when kept as pets. Two female rabbits is the best option as they are less aggressive than males. Provision of a weather-proof and rabbit/predator-proof enclosure in the playspace is essential for keeping these animals.

Composting and worm farms

Compost bins use kitchen scraps and garden waste to create rich compost for the garden. Children can experiment with the process of composting using sealed plastic bottles as mini composts to examine how long fruit and vegetables take to decompose. Worm farms are highly effective compost makers that include the added interest of worms which can consume their own body weight in a day. One Victorian school has multiple worm farms and they bottle the worm juice (urine) and sell it under the amusing name of 'Grange Wormatige'. Another school in New Zealand sells worm lollipops made from worm castings (poo!). A small ball of castings is placed in a square of muslin and secured with string, then a stick inserted so the lollipop can be easily pushed into the ground around plants that need extra nutrients. Various designs and sizes of timber or recycled plastic compost bins and worm farms are available from plant nurseries, local councils and environmental organisations.

Checkpoints for composting/worm farming:

- Be careful to avoid too much citrus as citrus is acidic and will slow the decomposition. Worms do not thrive in an acid worm farm.
- Meat, fish, dairy and bread should also be avoided as it can attract vermin to the area.
- Ensure the container is placed in an area with some light and some shade.
- Regularly check moisture levels.

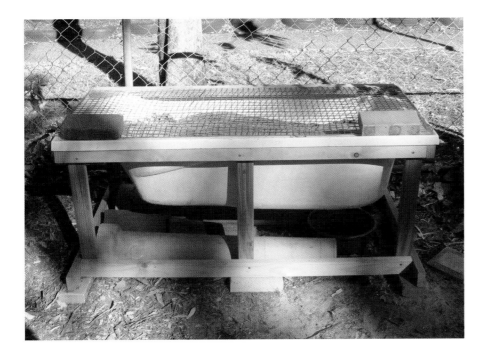

An old bathtub has been re-used as a worm farm at Campus Kindy, University of Queensland.

St Kilda and Balaclava Kindergarten includes multiple compost bins in the vegetable garden.

If the above checkpoints are a problem, then consider a new type of compost bin now available called aerobic bins. They are an ideal compost bin for children's centres because they are a sealed bin that contains a patented 'lung' or aeration core to promote rapid aerobic breakdown of organic matter. The aerobic process generates heat that breaks down the organic matter in as little as 12 weeks; also, this method of composting has reduced greenhouse gas emission. A centre would only need one bin that can be regularly topped up and this bin type copes with large amounts of citrus or bread scraps that are often abundant in children's centres. Theoretically, anything organic can be placed in the bin including branches and meat or dairy products and it does not need to be aerated with a pitchfork. The high temperature in the bin kills grass weeds and seeds, it is vermin/pet proof and the design includes a tap to release liquid fertiliser that can be poured onto garden beds.

Natural elements

The natural world offers a range of materials that provide open-ended play opportunities for children. Children need no instruction for using sand, mud, logs, stones or water.

Water features

Water is a universal natural play resource that children throughout the world enjoy; however, not every child has an abundance of water to use in play. We have all become more aware of the need to conserve water during recent droughts in Australia and water conservation is certainly a consideration in the natural playspace, along with other everyday sustainable practices. How much a centre restricts children's water play opportunities is a philosophical issue that will vary with the sociocultural context of the centre and its location. The benefits of water play are endless and water creates another connection between people, plants, animals and the land. However, it would be worthwhile consulting with local water and early childhood regulatory authorities before launching into a water feature development.

Rain water tanks
Rainwater tanks could almost be described as an essential resource for an early childhood centre in Australia. Many centres use rainwater for children's play and this may reduce the water available for play when the water runs out.

This Australian designed Waterwall ™ tank is incorporated into the fence line of St Kilda and Balaclava Kindergarten. Four have been installed and each tank holds 1000 litres of water.

This sends a powerful message to children about the origins of water and the water cycle. Many centres are now including multiple tanks that can be plumbed for water use inside buildings for flushing toilets or laundry purposes. Check your local phone directory for suppliers of water tanks.

Water courses

Water courses or trickle streams are used mostly with children aged 3–5 years. Successful designs include a pump that recycles the water through the course and serves two purposes: to conserve water and ensure the water collects in an enclosed secure pit when the pump is turned off. Safety is a prime consideration with any water experience and watercourses need to be situated in active areas where there is constant supervision. Materials such as rocks, trees, logs and plants create a naturalistic environment that is a delight to the senses, especially on a hot day.

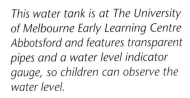

This water tank is at The University of Melbourne Early Learning Centre Abbotsford and features transparent pipes and a water level indicator gauge, so children can observe the water level.

This trickle stream design incorporates river pebbles and hardy plants. The significance of this feature is in the scale and textures to be discovered.

Attwood Child Care Centre and Kindergarten has a large watercourse that enables children to paddle and explore the differing levels over the length of the watercourse.

Water fountains

Many commercially made water fountains such as rock bubblers or water bowls are inexpensive and add the soothing sound of tricking water or aesthetic beauty to the playspace. A solar pump obtained from a plant nursery or solar supplier can also be used to explore solar energy.

This inexpensive water bowl adds aesthetic beauty to the playspace at The University of Melbourne Early Learning Centre Abbotsford.

Sandpits

Sandpits are essential fixtures in playspaces for infants, toddlers and pre-school aged children where skills build from sensory exploration to complex play constructing deep holes, bridges, roadways and waterways. Ensure that the depth of sand is sufficient for the most accomplished hole diggers! The Playground and Recreation Association of Victoria suggests a depth of approximately 600 mm. It is helpful if the sandpit is located near a tap or water tank for easy access to water and effective drainage is essential. Timber surrounds or decking can provide a place for play and/or propping. Sandpits need shade due to the high reflectivity of sand and the often contemplative or stationary type play that occurs in sand. Climbing plants on a timber frame or nearby deciduous trees provide natural shade options (refer to Chapter 5 for sun protection). Sand needs to be kept away from grassed areas and plants, as these will suffocate under spreading sand.

The Lady Gowrie Child Centre Melbourne sandpit includes defined sections for different play possibilities.

Mud patches

Playing with mud is as vital as sand and water in an early childhood program. Mud has different qualities and textures that enable children to use it wet or dry, for mudpies, cooking, digging trenches and creating roadways. Mud can be moulded in a way that sand cannot, creating a sensory experience for infants

The mud patch at Lady Gowrie Child Centre Melbourne enables children to be physically active in a large well designed space—digging, mud play and transportation of mud in wheelbarrows.

and toddlers and creative challenge for older children. Many adults reflect on their childhoods and remember the joy of making mudpies. Mud patches work well if they are big enough, 12 square metres is a good size. Digging patches are often square or rectangle with wooden edges, however irregular shapes with natural rock or plant borders create a less rigid and more naturalistic mud patch. If purchasing soil from a plant nursery, local council or building supplier for a mud patch, mix in approximately one-third sand to two-thirds soil to promote a more friable and therefore, diggable mix. Mud patches do require regular turning over to ensure they are diggable for children.

Logs, boulders, rocks and stones

Natural materials such as logs, boulders, rocks and stones add inexpensive design features to the playspace. Logs can be used for seating, boulders create interesting climbing challenges that mirror nature and gravel pits provide textured variations of ground surfaces. Children can spend lengthy periods of time moving the gravel, logs and stones around, thus feeling a sense of empowerment within the playspace. Note that a range of gravel and stone sizes can be used, but give careful consideration to potential choking hazards and physical lifting challenges when selecting an appropriate size. Plant nurseries, local councils or parents may be able to provide these materials.

This gravel pit at The University of Melbourne Early Learning Centre Abbotsford provides open-ended play and a sense of real work, the two children pictured spent hours moving the loose materials around.

Source logs from local councils for seats and feature areas (Campus Kindy, University of Queensland).

This space was transformed from an unwanted sandpit to a dry creek bed filled with rocks and stones at Lady Gowrie Child Centre Melbourne.

Plants

Planting can enrich the child's play environment more than any other element. The more varied it is the richer the sensory experience ... The combination of good planting and a sensitive teacher will enable young children to enjoy and learn more, as they pick, observe, collect, sort, arrange, tend, water, plant, propagate and prune (Walsh, 1991, p 25).

Trees

A balance of deciduous and evergreen trees is the backbone of any garden. Deciduous trees provide shade and dappled light in warmer months and lose their leaves in the winter allowing sun to enter the playspace. Increasingly, children's services cover the playspace in shade cloth without considering the many benefits of trees. Trees provide plant materials such as cones, bark, leaves and branches for craft and play; they provide learning opportunities as children can observe seasonal changes and patterns in the trees; and trees provide a natural ground cover or mulch.

The University of Melbourne Early Learning Centre Abbotsford playspace incorporates climbing ropes and swings attached to a large stable tree. Children are able to experience calculated risk and challenge.

Shrubs

Shrubs that grow to 1 or 2 metres are excellent mid-level plants to create wind-breaks, divided play areas or provide a dense backdrop for secluded play. The shrubs can become crucial to the play if toy animals are hidden in the foliage, sheets are attached to low branches during cubby construction or peep-holes are found though the bushes. Many shrubs or small trees also provide scented flowers or fruit such as gooseberry bushes, lily pillies or dwarf fruit trees.

Fruit and vegetable gardens

Many centres may install a garden and successfully grow plants, but are children actively involved in the process? Growing and propagating plants, harvesting, cooking or preparing food and then eating the produce are all learning opportunities. Children need to be actively involved in the life cycle of plants to develop connections with nature. Vegetables above and below the ground can be grown all year. Potatoes, carrots, capsicums, peas, beans, lettuce, tomatoes and cucumbers are easily grown examples. Successful fruit plants will depend on climate: tropical areas can grow paw paw, hot climates are suitable for oranges whilst cooler climates can grow apples, pears and plums. Strawberries are very successful in most Australian climates and fruiting vines such as passionfruit or kiwi fruit add diversity. According to region, centres might also investigate the potential of indigenous food plants.

Established trees provide a frame to the smaller plants. Trees and shrubs can create a barrier from busy roads. Consider using mature trees, they are worth the investment. These deciduous trees promote seasonal observations and provide leaves for play and investigation.

St Kilda and Balaclava Kinder-garten had a wooden boat that was starting to fall apart. They did not want to throw it away and chose to embed the boat into the ground and build a herb and vegetable garden. Children and families experience a visual reminder that objects we may be inclined to throw away can be used in alternative ways.

Indigenous gardens

Indigenous plantings that attract wildlife such as birds, bees and butterflies can be a significant part of a natural playspace. A local nursery, council or horticulture group could supply information about indigenous or local plants for particular areas. Not all Australian native plants are suitable for all parts of Australia. Tim Low (2003) author, biologist and environmental activist, expresses great concern about planting Australian plants that are not indigenous to the area. Plants that are indigenous to your local area are the ones you should focus on. The distance between Perth and Sydney is approximately the distance between Portugal and Russia. You would never refer to a Russian plant as a native plant in Portugal and yet this is what we do with Australian native plants. Using indigenous plants ensures that the biodiversity of plants is maintained along with the wildlife that needs them to survive.

Mainly indigenous plants were selected to attract native butterflies to St Leonards Cornish Campus.

Grass seats

Living plants such as grass, or soft ground covers such as scented thyme and Corsican mint, or shade loving native violets (Viola hederacea), can be planted in containers and used as seats or play surfaces. This is an ideal way of bringing plants to a barren outside playspace that may have minimal or no natural plants (Young and Elliott, 2003). It is important to replenish, rest or replant the seat over time as it will become compacted with lots of sitting!

Hanging baskets, planter boxes and potted plants

Planting in containers is an ideal way to add plants to barren landscapes that may have few plants or garden beds. Hanging baskets need hardy plants as they dry out quickly. Containers of bright annuals such as nasturtiums, lobelia, petunias, geraniums or herbs soften the playspace adding colours, smells and textures. Small trees and shrubs can be planted in tubs to improve the aesthetic appeal as well as to divide or screen specific play areas.

This idea for grass seats progressed from plastic pots to these beautiful wooden benches. A parent at St Kilda and Balaclava Kindergarten made them from hardwood, with a hollow metal tray inside with draining holes. The benches are light enough to move around, but sturdy enough for seats or dividers.

Hanging baskets of bright annuals soften the walls in this infant play-space at Keysborough Community Children's Centre.

Herbs can be easily grown in planter boxes. This centre uses planter pots as dividers to provide aesthetic appeal and aromatic plants to the toddler playground at Keysborough Community Children's Centre.

A simple pot of flowering annuals adds appeal to this outside table at the University of Melbourne Early Learning Centre Abbotsford.

Conclusion

A well designed outdoor playspace needs to be a reflection of the local community as well as meeting the sociocultural needs of the families, children and staff that use the space. This is a frequently expressed value, but what does this actually mean in practice? It means that a childcare centre in Darwin will consider different design features to a kindergarten in Melbourne. The plants and materials available in every region will vary according to changes in weather and the geographic landscape. Incorporate local plants, stones, ground covers and opportunities to discover animals. Invite local gardeners, carpenters, artists and crafts people to contribute boulders, stonework, logs, garden features, artworks, mosaics and sculptures for the playspace. Outside spaces become both rich learning environments and places of aesthetic beauty that encourage adults and children to want to spend time in them. Particularly if they become a microcosm of the positive features of local communities, a miniature world for children to explore, a miniature world with endless possibilities, a miniature world that fosters connections with nature.

> A playground should be like a small-scale replica of the world, with as many as possible of the sensory experiences to be found in the world included in it. Experiences for every sense are needed, for instance: rough and smooth objects to look at and feel; light and heavy things to pick up; water and wet materials as well as dry things; cool materials and materials warmed by the sun; soft and hard surfaces; things that make sounds (running water) or that can be struck, plucked, plinked, etc; smells of all varieties (flowers, bark, mud); shiny bright objects and dull, dark ones; things both huge and tiny; high and low places to look at; materials of every type, natural, synthetic, thin, thick, and so on. The list is inexhaustible, and the larger the number of items that are included, the richer and more varied the environment for the child (Dattner quoted in Greenman, 1988, p 177).

Acknowledgment

A range of early childhood services have been sourced for ideas and photographs and the author wishes to acknowledge the many services who have generously shared their innovative designs and ideas.

Website resources

Australian Native Bee Centre
www.zeta.org.au/~anbrc/

Global Garden
www.globalgarden.com.au

RSPCA
www.rspcavic.org/animal_care/small_animal_care.htm

References

Corkery L, 1987, *Playspace. Handbook for Planning Outdoor Play Environments*, Community Activities Network, NSW.

Greenman J, 1988, *Caring Spaces, Learning Spaces Children's Environments that Work*, Exchange Press Inc, Redmond WA, USA.

Jeffers S, 1991, *Brother Eagle, Sister Sky*, Puffin Books, The Penguin Group. London.

Low T, 2003, *The New Nature. Winners and Losers in Wild Australia*, Penguin Books, Australia.

Louv R, 2005, *The Last Child in the Woods. Saving our Children from Nature Deficit Disorder*, Algonquin Books, USA.

Nabhan GP and Trimble S, 1994, *The Geography of Childhood. Why Children Need Wild Places*, Beacon Press, Boston, USA.

Payne P, 1998, 'Children's Conceptions of Nature', *Australian Journal of Environmental Education*. Vol 14, pp 19–26.

Suzuki D and Vanderlinden K, 1999, *You are the Earth*, Allen and Unwin, St Leonards NSW, Australia.

Walsh P, 1991, *Early Childhood Playgrounds. Planning an Outside Learning Environment*, Pademelon Press, Sydney, Australia.

Young T and Elliott S, 2003, *Just Discover. Connecting Young Children with the Natural World*, Tertiary Press, Melbourne.

Bibliography

CSIRO, 1986, *Earthworms for Gardeners and Fishermen*, CSIRO Publishing Collingwood, Australia.

Cushing H, 2001, *The ABC Book of Gardening for Kids*, Australian Broadcasting Commission, Sydney.

Durie J, 2005, *Outdoor Kids A Practical Guide for Kids in the Garden*, Jamie Durie Publishing, Crows Nest NSW.

French J, 1993, *The Chook Book*, Aird Books, Flemington, Australia.

Matthews C, 2002, *Great Gardens for Kids*, Hamlyn, London.

Starbuck S, Olthof M and Midden K, 2002, *Hollyhocks and Honeybees, Garden Projects for Young Children*, Redleaf Press, Minnesota.

Woodrow L, 1996, *The Permaculture Home Garden*, Penguin Books, Australia.

How do natural playspaces meet developmental needs and

interests?

Kerry Rogers

4

Introduction

Whenever I try to pinpoint the value of a natural environment as a foundation for an early childhood program, the word 'dynamic' always comes to mind. An outdoor space that has the elements of nature, changing weather conditions, the growth and demise of vegetation and the manoeuvrability of the 'loose parts' (and the not so 'loose parts') means that the playspace changes both gradually and suddenly and sometimes unexpectedly. These changes bring an element of surprise and wonder to children's experiences and challenges for problem solving. The flexibility of natural elements allows for individual interpretation of how they may be used and the natural flow from one element to the other encourages an integration of play across a range of developmental areas and play styles.

A sandpit with rock surrounds may be set with logs and dinosaurs where 5-year-olds are engaged in imaginative play. A mulched pathway adjacent to the sandpit may lead to a grassy mound on which a small group of toddlers might be blowing bubbles in the breeze. As the bubbles float over the sandpit the children may use the dinosaurs to catch the bubbles. Then, 3-year-olds moving prams along the path can become engaged in language about the event they have stumbled upon.

*Imaginative sand play
with dinosaurs.*

This chapter will explore the value of natural playspaces and provide ideas for developmentally based experiences that utilise the 'dynamic' of natural playspaces. It will integrate a range of elements that impact on programming for children—to not only provide for the varying stages and domains of development, but also allow flexibility to meet a range of needs and interests and allow early childhood educators to explore a range of curriculum approaches. These environments—with their opportunities for open ended experiences, exploration, risk taking and complex play—provide a challenge to children's sense of enquiry while inviting opportunities to connect with nature.

> A natural setting has the degree of complexity, plasticity and manipulability which allows a child to experience many developmentally significant play behaviours, such as role playing, cause-effect actions, constructive play etc (Kirkby, 1989, p 7).

From a developmental perspective, early childhood educators traditionally divide early childhood into *under three's* and *over three's*. Although this traditional approach may need to be challenged, this somewhat arbitrary division is used here simply because children's centres, government regulations and standards still apply this approach and most early childhood educators are planning within these parameters.

The child—Birth–3 years

There is obviously a vast developmental range in this age group and safety issues must be considered when planning. Natural playspaces that include mud, soil, mulch, gravel, and so on, can pose a health and safety risk to very young children. Mouthing is a necessary part of a child's learning about their world and stumbling and falling are frequent occurrences. However, a supportive adult can modify environments and encourage safe use of play materials. Babies would rather eat sand than stir a cooking pot, but with an adult to distract and engage them, modelling safe ways of using materials; these very young children can enjoy the benefit of what is otherwise known as unsuitable play. Adults have a very significant role with this age group in natural playspaces both role modelling and sharing the wonder and aesthetics of natural elements.

Recent brain research reinforces the importance of positive experiences in infancy and toddlerhood. Normal brain development is dependent on specific patterns of experience at specific times of development and most of the critical periods are in the early years. 'If the required experience is not forthcoming at the critical time, later experience may not be able to ameliorate the negative affects on brain functioning' (Rolfe, 2000a, p 9).

Self-image that is shaped and reshaped as individuals react with each other and the environment is a lifetime process, but is influenced greatly by the experiences in early childhood. A positive sense of self contributes not only to brain development, but to the development of resilience, the ability to 'bounce back' from life's disappointments. '… [T]he feelings of autonomy, initiative, competence and self esteem comes from their ability to promote within children a view of themselves as agents with control over their lives and their destiny' (Rolfe, 2000b, p 12).

Natural playspaces, where children are encouraged to be in control of themselves and their environment, to develop skills of their own choice at their own pace and to feel honoured for their achievements, allow for children to view themselves as 'agents with control'. This positive sense of self is one of the prime goals of infant and toddler programs.

Babies

Babies develop an initial sense of self through a partnership between themselves and one or more loving adults. The most important element for babies

Younger children enjoy the close company of adults.

in a natural playspace is an adult who will share a sense of wonder in the breeze, the flowers in the garden and will do some risk taking on the child's behalf such as holding a small garden creature. This loving rapport provides positive feedback to the child that the adult values them and their sense of self becomes a positive one.

Babies are both aware of and fascinated by sounds and movement, so listening to the scrunch of dry leaves, watching birds in the trees overhead, feeling wind on their face and the sensation of grass on their hands are constant sensory stimuli. Adults can add to the natural sights and sounds by providing mobiles that blow in the breeze and wind chimes that tinkle when they touch as well as a variety of colours in plantings, rugs and cushions.

A sheltered place for scrunching autumn leaves at Berwick Kindergarten.

Grassy open spaces are ideal for babies (mulched areas pose a choking threat) as they can be laid on blankets to watch the play of other children as well as experience natural elements but, once mobile, they have space to crawl and explore further. Sawn off tree trunks and smooth logs that are positioned and secured to ensure stability provide supports for pulling themselves up and clambering over. Small rises and slopes will provide another dimension to the challenge of mobility as children need to employ more complex balance and perceptual skills to negotiate these areas.

Baby play that is mostly repetitive and functional, such as spooning sand into a bowl and tipping it out, is a process often repeated with great glee. This is an ideal opportunity for the adult to engage with the child and respond with delight to their game.

Toddlers

As children become upright and mobile they need opportunities to test and strengthen their loco-motor skills. Open grassy spaces are needed to run, to chase bubbles in the wind, to dance and to push and pull.

Children of this age group eagerly participate in clambering and crawling through type activities and adults can provide challenges with logs to climb over, mounds to roll down and tunnels in shrubbery to crawl through. As falls from these low clambering over spaces are rarely heavy impact, any additional low equipment pieces required can be positioned on grass or soft mulch, even fine gravel. This allows toddler set ups to be located safely away from the more structured climbing spaces that may be being used by older children.

The toddler strives for independence and is developing autonomy, often testing limits while still being pulled back to dependence. Toddlers want to move away from the adult, but like to keep them in sight. Pathways that meander through the playspace, perhaps over a low bridge, allow children to pull trolleys, push prams, ride wheel toys and feel as though they are moving away from the adult, but they are still able to have the adult in sight if needed. Natural playspaces with items that can be manipulated allow the toddler to feel independent and in control—to move a small log, to cart mud and sand away, and so on.

Bubbles to chase!

Cause and effect fascinates this age group and they explore thoroughly and in their own way. Flexibility and a sense of humour are essential when planning for the toddler.

A playspace set with baskets of puppets and books on a mat in a quiet area, pine cones and large tip trucks in the sand, and a water tray with jugs and basins for pouring gives a clear message to adults of the purpose of the setting. However, it may only take ten minutes of creative and active exploration on the part of the toddler to find children carrying the baskets loaded with pine cones to dump in the water, watching them bob then float; to loading the books into the tip trucks and watching as they slide out into the sandpit; to carrying jugs of water to the nearest immobile child and pouring the water over them awaiting the results of their actions. Energy is also essential when planning for the toddler.

A re-used bottle for dropping stones and pieces of driftwood into, a sensory and fine motor experience for toddlers fascinated by cause and effect.

A re-used carton for arranging collected pine cones; what other ways might a toddler use them?

Language develops rapidly during the toddler stage and children need opportunities for listening to language and experimenting with sounds. Clusters of tree stumps, large smooth rocks, logs and bushy alcoves provide a small group space for impromptu music and language groups. Children can come and go and can control the amount of participation they wish to have. Also, follow the leader games such as singing songs and playing instruments or creative movement experiences such as jungle walks and train songs can meander around pathways, through shrubbery, and under archways.

The flexibility of natural playspaces provides support for the social emotional development of the toddler. Although most are still solitary in their play they begin to enjoy the company of others in parallel, playing at the same experience, but focused only on their own play, with no engagement or sharing of ideas or equipment. A group of toddlers gathered around a tree stump may all be engaged in mud 'cooking', but each will have their own bowl and spoon to stir ingredients and will be using language mostly to themselves or to the adult (who then will need to taste each individual offering).

Toddlers often move as a group—all in the sand before all 'herding' off to 'ride on the train'. Although they are learning to play alongside other children, the toddler may use aggression to solve problems and needs help to take turns.

In natural playspaces, the props for play are readily available, so adults generally do not need to limit numbers of children engaged in play as in more structured playspaces. Adults can easily provide both sufficient space and equipment to keep all children engaged in a natural playspace. For example, in a structured playspace where the 'boat' is an adult designed structure with four seats and one steering wheel, eight 2-year-olds will have difficulty managing the disappointment of missing out on the 'first turn'. However, if the boat is an old cardboard box and the steering wheel is a plastic reel, adults can always provide extra boxes and reels, so that all children are invited to participate.

Toddlers are beginning to pretend and to imitate. Alcoves cut into shrubbery provide places where adults can set up spaces for two or three children to play alongside each other. Teddies, baskets and blankets; cooking sets with leaves, gum nuts and sawdust; or individual sand basins (basins set into tyres are ideal) with plastic animals, leaves and pine cones are but a few examples. Just be prepared for the fact that these materials may not always stay in the one space given that the toddlers love carting and hauling.

Staff in a 3- to 4-year-olds program had thoughtfully prepared a playspace with several large dinosaurs, some branches, mulch, and pinecones to develop some interactive play for the children. Before the children came outside, the toddlers came to visit. Within 10 minutes the dinosaurs had all disappeared. A discerning scan of the play area revealed all the toddlers playing in the sand, painting, riding bikes, each with one large dinosaur tucked under one arm!

The advantage of natural playspaces that provide many permanent imaginative spaces, is that the children can engage in imaginative play in a space of their choice—uncut grass, a muddy corner, or the garden. Also, hardy, low, dense planting can provide a landscape for imaginative play; for example, violets or other ground covers. Place some elephants, dinosaurs or teddies amongst dense planting along with some smooth logs or tree rounds and the toddlers can use the natural foliage and surroundings to develop their play.

By providing lots of baskets and things to collect—pine cones, leaves, gum nuts, seed pods—adults can meet the toddlers need to collect, carry and dump. By using natural materials, any items not collected at the end of play will do no damage to the environment, will not deteriorate in the rain and will not cause a litter problem.

Water play provides sensory experiences and opportunities to explore cause and effect vital to this age group. Grass areas or natural groundcover are ideal spaces for setting multiple water containers at the child's level, preferably flat on the ground, so children can move around and transfer water from container to container. Any spills provide water for the lawn or garden. Many watering cans are needed for this age group and they will also enjoy water painting with buckets and paint brushes. A water tank with child accessible taps will support their growing independence too.

Sand is also a multi-faceted experience for children, providing not just a sensory experience, but also a material with which to practise imitative roles and develop parallel play, to stir a cooking pot or offer a cup of tea to an adult. By providing multiples of cooking pots, large spoons, cups, saucers and serving plates, children are able to imitate the familiar domestic scenes

A bowl placed in a tyre and filled with water provides an effective water play experience.

in the company of other children. By adding water to vary the consistency of the sand plus some pine cones, gum nuts and pebbles for decoration, the children will be extending their symbolic thinking and gradually move into more complex play.

Much of the toddler's time in a natural playspace will be locating, identifying and generally manipulating small creatures. Just try to garden with toddlers! On the discovery of the first and every subsequent worm all play must stop, so everyone can discuss, touch, observe and of course search for more so that every child has one! The more natural and nurtured the playspaces are, the greater variety of wildlife they will attract. Interest in living things not only provides opportunity to learn about growth, development and life cycles; it is also an introduction to children that we share the environment with other creatures and have a responsibility to support their survival. It provides adults with an opportunity to explore feelings and the beginnings of empathy for other living things.

Flowers also offer an interest as children can smell and pick these. The toddler will mostly finger and manipulate these as they learn about flora the only way a toddler can—actively. However, with an adult showing respect and conservation of the specimens, the child will soon learn to also be aware of the consequences of picking living things and use them respectfully.

Implications for planning—Birth to 3-year-olds

The table below provides an overview of some of the developmental characteristics you can expect to observe when planning for the birth to 3-year-old age group. Also listed are planning considerations for the types of playspaces that we need to provide to support development and some safety points.

DEVELOPMENTAL CHARACTERISTICS			PLANNING CONSIDERATIONS	
Social/Emotional	Language/Cognitive	Physical	Playspace	Safety
Solitary play moves to associative play.	Repetitive and functional play develops into imitative play and some role play.	Spatial awareness is limited.	Spaces for adults to prop to support play, ensure safety and excite.	Adults to supervise the use of materials equipment & space.
Sharing is not an option.	Learning is hands on and cause and effect based.	Mobility develops and gait is slowly refined.	Grassy spaces for chasing, low clambering equipment.	Multiples of equipment to avoid aggressive problem solving.
Independence is developing but frequently reverts to dependence, separation from parents can be difficult.	Thinking is egocentric.	Senses are used to explore objects.	Pathways for pushing and pulling wheel toys.	Moveable barriers— logs, plant pots, hay bales to protect smaller children.

DEVELOPMENTAL CHARACTERISTICS			PLANNING CONSIDERATIONS	
Social/Emotional	Language/Cognitive	Physical	Playspace	Safety
Growing need for autonomy and control can lead to tantrums.	All senses are actively engaged in learning.	Large muscle activity dominates— running, sliding, rolling etc.	Sheltered alcoves for safely placing babies on rugs, or books or instruments.	Water containers are emptied when not in supervised use.
Change can be difficult to manage.	Verbal language is developing and increases rapidly.	Environments are actively explored.	Variety of smaller sand spaces as well as water opportunities.	Toxicity and allergies need to be taken into account when selecting plants.
	Aggression frequently used for problem solving.		Gardens that provide touch, smell and visual stimuli.	
	Attention spans are short.			

The 3- to 5-Year-Old

Often referred to as the Preschool Years, this is the time the child moves from being a solitary and egocentric concrete thinker to develop into a co-operative, empathetic individual with increasing ability to use symbolic thought processes and think in abstract ways. Language becomes directed to each other rather than to the adult and co-ordination develops as children refine their physical skills into testing out their abilities and doing stunts. Peers become important and play becomes both complex and co-operative.

3-year-olds

Three-year-olds are still learning through their senses and their developing concentration spans allow adults to introduce sensory experiences into their increasingly interactive dramatic and imaginative play. For example, sand play using water, gum nuts and twigs, cooking with sawdust, mud, mulch or leaves and bathing babies or washing dolls clothes on the lawn provides complexity to their play.

Although concentration spans are increasing, 3-year-olds can be very distractible, flitting to every new activity that catches their eye. In a natural landscape that provides gardens, logs and structures to delineate spaces, young children are not so exposed to the peripheral activity around them, but rather sheltered in garden 'rooms'. Planned and spontaneous experiences can utilise many of the existing natural features and so don't call to the child 'come see what's here'.

Three-year-olds now begin to play out roles. Mostly these are the ones familiar to them; for example, home, travelling, animals, centre routines. The advantage of children being able to develop role play in a natural setting using open-ended materials is that the children are able to interpret the environment and props to represent their own cultural perspective. A cluster of tree trunks can provide dining in a restaurant, in front of television, at a kitchen bench or on the floor. Small stones, weed clumps, gum nuts and leaves can be dim sims, fish fingers, pasta or falafel. In this way, each child, no matter what their cultural background, can draw on their own experience to extend their play. Would this be possible if we set up a table and chairs, brought out the home corner stove and provided knives and forks, then presented the children with the 'faux' food of plastic fried eggs, hamburgers and chips?

> *In a centre with a large number of Laotion families, the children played repeatedly in the home corner—admittedly pretty mainstream, but with natural coloured playdough. The play was intense and animated with the same theme appeared to be repeated daily, the cutting up and dishing out of the playdough very much resembling 'father' dishing up and serving the Sunday Roast. On the day the Laotian aide was able to engage in the play, she explained that the children were in fact 'slaughtering a pig'. Evidently the practice in that community was for the clan to purchase whole pigs, slaughter them and divide them up. Would the same quality of imagination, role play and theme development have occurred if the environment was set with plastic bacon and eggs?*

Although language is now moving ahead in leaps and bounds, 3-year-olds are still concrete thinkers and discussions still need to focus on the here and now—planting seeds, weeding the garden, hauling soil and compost. Discussing possums in the tree, bird nests and mobiles blowing in the wind will provide richer language exchange than discussing a story or what they did on the weekend.

For children who are just moving into group situations at this stage, such as a 3-year-old kindergarten program, the natural outdoor playspace provides a secure and soothing space to adjust to life (albeit for a few hours) without a parent and in a large group. An area that has spaces to sit alone and observe (without a well-meaning adult taking you by the hand to join in) provides time for the child to adjust to a new situation.

As early childhood educators, our main role in supporting the transition from home to centre life is to maintain that feeling of uniqueness, while learning about being part of a group of other equally unique and special people. A natural environment where children are able to make choices for themselves and have control of their play is fundamental to the transitioning child of whatever age, to feel that their uniqueness is valued.

4-year-olds

Four-year-olds are inquisitive and want to find out about their world. They show an interest in natural science and simple technology. They ask many questions but, unlike 3-year-olds that ask a lot of questions without necessarily being interested in listening to the answer, 4-year-olds really do want to know. By providing containers for collecting natural specimens and magnifying glasses and by having reference books readily available, small discussion groups can spontaneously be provided for. These groups can happen on a log, on a deck, a rug on the ground, standing around a tree stump or sitting on the side of a mound.

The dynamic and ever changing nature of natural playspaces means there is always work to be done. Children of all ages love to 'help', but 4-year-olds find genuine value in developing their own real projects—digging a drain, making an elephant patch, building a frog pond or constructing a bird feeder. This work provides opportunities to challenge problem-solving skills, introduce technology such as levers and pulleys, explore maths skills such as measuring and estimating, and language skills such as making lists and signs.

A donkey type water pump provides a simple technology experience for four-year-olds at Berwick Kindergarten.

A muddy elephant patch nestled in grass thickets for imaginative play at Berwick Kindergarten.

Four-year-old play has moved from domestic themes modelled on familiar adults to more removed subjects such as community workers. This is also the time for superhero and rough and tumble play. A natural landscape offers complexity to explore the play theme options. There will always be trees to

Problem solving with a pulley.

Some logs in the shrubbery just waiting for exploration at Berwick Kindergarten.

A jungle like shrubbery with potential for hideouts at Berwick Kindergarten.

'catch fire', shops to be 'robbed' of their pine cone supplies and jungles for dangerous animals to be lurking. Shrubbery provides hideouts; tree logs and mounds convert to 'look outs'; all of this stretching children's imagination and abstract thinking far more than a built cubby, fire fighters pole or miniature grocery packets.

Peer relationships are now becoming important so children need soothing and private spaces—some well positioned seating, smooth rocks, or tree stumps to retire to, either with a new found friend or alone to adjust to rejection.

This is the age of the 'cubby'. A ready built cubby is often the space for the first three children to get in and spend all their time keeping others out. Even if children do develop themes in these structures, they are often unable to extend the play outside the cubby because once they leave the space it will be commandeered by others.

Sheer material turns a platform into a cubby.

Kylin (2003, p 21) investigated children's perspectives of enclosures or 'dens'. Although this exploration involved children 9–13 years, she concluded 'the common factor in the experience of the den as a social and secret place is the sense of control that children feel they have, both over the den as a physical space and over the other children who share the den'.

A playspace that provides multiple spaces for cubby building either in bushy areas, bark over A-frames or sheets over tree branches, allows all children to have access to a retreat area and to take ownership of their space over a period of time. This allows them to then further develop their play by moving out and extending the play scenario or integrating with other children and other play themes.

One particularly hot day, when even the shaded playground of the 4-year-old kindergarten would have been uncomfortable, staff quickly cleaned up an area opening off the playroom which had previously been used for rubbish, recycling and storage. This area had several scrubby trees, some lawn but, importantly, shade and a reasonably cool breeze. Initially staff planned to set up construction sets on rugs for some passive play that they deemed suitable for such a hot day. However what eventuated was very different.

The children, delighted to be in an area that was normally 'off limits', surveyed the area of scrubby trees, sparse lawn, dirt and concrete and announced they wanted to make cubbies. Away went the construction sets and out came the cubby play equipment—sheets, pegs, mats, cooking/camping props and the children built a total of four cubbies.

These were so close that some of the 'walls' were co joined. Instead of this resulting in conflictual play as children were crowding each other's playspace, the amount of cooperative engagement was amazing. They were borrowing cooking equipment, sharing barbeques, making tunnels into each other's cubbies and offering advice on repairs and adjustments. The play continued to evolve and become more complex throughout the day with one cubby reserved for 'resting' with books and cushions (it really was a hot day!).

5-year-olds

Five-year-olds are self-resourcing, relatively responsible individuals. They like to help and respond to praise. They are more sure of themselves and less likely to boast. Adults become like a co-worker/co-learner to the 5- and 6-year-old.

Five-year-olds value group acceptance and prefer co-operative play. Their play now increases in complexity, not only developing themes, but using symbols, and acting out roles, with ongoing verbal interactions and the sharing of ideas. The play may continue over many days with increasingly complex themes and plots.

This sociodramatic play is considered to be one of the highest forms of play in childhood.

Sociodramatic play prepares a child for many of life's experiences. The representational skills practiced in sociodramatic play are essential to the child's ability to conceptualize many of the things taught in school. Reading deals with symbols for language, numerical symbols represent quantities of objects, and science uses molecules to stand for the unseen. The interactions of a child in play prepare her for the give-and-take of

social relationships. Creativity is strengthened as a child resolves dilemmas and expands on situations that lead to new ways to play (Smilansky, 1968 quoted in Heidemann and Hewitt, 1990, p 12).

Natural environments provide for the continuity of this important play in that the props needed—trees to hide in, hideouts made of shrubbery, bridges of logs, campfires of pine cones and so on, do not have to be packed away each night and play can continue. Complexity can increase as the log that was the bridge one-day could be the dragon the next. Space is maximised as other children may be using these same props either at the same time or at other times during the day as something completely different. The log 'bridge' may be a train for some 3-year-olds, toddlers may collect the pinecones to haul, and the bush hideout may also serve the purpose of a bear cave for 4-year-olds.

Dense bamboo planting, a place to explore and test independence at Knoxfield Preschool.

The increase in their abstract thinking abilities enables 5-year-olds to question and wonder and to find out things. They like to collate their knowledge and to display for all to see. There is always somewhere in a well-planned natural playspace—for example, tree trunks, small paved areas set into raised garden beds, timber edging of playspaces—for children to display their findings. Adults can support these findings with appropriate reference books, clipboards with discussion notes or gather a group of children around and talk about their 'find'.

Five-year-olds are not always content with just a 'cubby'. The growing independence of the 5-year-old requires not just privacy, but also distance. They like to pack up everything and take off 'camping'. A natural playspace will usually have an area where children can actually remove themselves and feel they are really out of our sight and really responsible for their own play, thus providing them with an opportunity to test their independence and our trust.

A challenging tree to practise climbing skills.

This is also a time when children may take things and lie about it. Given that this age group is fond of their teachers and carers, any indiscretions may weigh heavily on their conscience. They don't show their feelings quite as readily as in their younger years, so adults don't always know what is going on in the mind of this older child. Feelings of guilt may be brewing and some quiet spaces for a child to sit and chat with a trusted adult may help to clear the mind. The 'propping' spaces so valuable for adults working with babies also serve the purpose of a 'heart to heart' with a 5-year-old.

They like to do stunts and take risks. Trees with soft fall underneath, ropes and rope ladders, flying foxes and challenging climbing arrangements engage exuberant groups of 5-year-olds testing their skills. Now that competition has crept into the their lives, some sports events—races, ball games, hurdles—can be held.

A space for a stage or amphitheatre built into the playspace allows for a circus to be planned and performed and concerts to be rehearsed. They enjoy more structured games and some will delight in learning simple folk dances.

A stage and seating area with performance and dramatic play opportunities at Sunningdale Early Childhood Centre in the City of Hume.

The real work of the 4-year-old now can become long-term planned projects, as the 5-year-old likes to plan and research, use real tools and, more importantly, complete a task. The process is no longer good enough for the 5-year-old. They want the product too.

Because natural environments are ever changing and flexible there is always space for an ongoing project—a hanging rack for garden tools, a garden seat for visiting adults, a path to the compost bin. Photographs and diagrams of the progress can be collated and displayed by the children. Their pride in their achievements and contribution to their playspace really consolidates the feelings of self worth and ownership.

Implications for planning—3- to 5-year-olds

The table below provides an overview of some of the developmental characteristics you can expect to observe when planning for the 3- to 5-year-old age group. Also listed are planning considerations for the types of playspaces that we need to provide to support development and some safety points.

DEVELOPMENTAL CHARACTERISTICS			PLANNING CONSIDERATIONS	
Social/Emotional	Language/Cognitive	Physical	Playspace	Safety
Real work is important.	Language becomes a tool for social and peer relationships.	Physical skills of skipping, galloping, hopping are refined.	Dramatic play-spaces of tree trunks, logs, decks.	Ensure quality of softfall and fall zones for larger bodies and dare-devil psyches.
Social play becomes inter-active as children move from para-llel play.	Why? How? When? What? are frequently asked questions.	Eye/hand and eye/foot co-ordination develops.	Gardens that can be worked on, developed and evolve.	Supervise and teach safe handling of real tools.
Empathetic behaviour slowly replaces ego-centric behaviour.	Thinking processes become more abstract.	Stunts and feats of daring demonstrate increasing competence.	Spaces to act as tabletops for displaying 'finds'.	
Emotions become more controlled.	Displaying and articulating knowledge is important.	Spatial awareness is refined.	Trees for ropes, ladders and climbing.	
Independence and autonomy develop.	Interest in numbers and letters develop.	Fine motor skills and small muscle develop-ment increase.	Challenging climbing struc-tures for testing out skills and showing off stunts.	
Many fears are tested out through play themes and chasing games.	Knowledge of the world around them increases.		Shrubby spaces for cubbies.	
Cubby building features in play.	Interests and play themes move through domestic to community workers to fantasy themes and some superhero play.		Stage areas for performances.	
Peer group accep-tance becomes important.			Storage area for real work tools and materials.	
			Open spaces for ball games and running games.	
			Variety spaces for imaginative play—pebbles, fernery, desert.	

Conclusion

One of the advantages of a natural environment for meeting the developmental needs and interests of children is that the open-endedness of the structures, materials and props allow for large variation in skill and knowledge. Each child will find both challenge and achievement within the playspace.

As well, the excitement that nature inevitably brings to a child's life—the fluttering of a butterfly, leaves falling into the sandpit, finding a hiding dinosaur in the fernery, all add to the motivation to inquire, experiment and risk take. It gives us so many 'teachable moments' every day.

However, I believe the most valuable aspect of the natural learning environment is that, because it engages children so totally, the demands on adults for setting up, supervising and managing behaviour are lessened. We have time to really observe, understand and engage with the children to develop a mutual love of learning outdoors.

References

Dahlberg G, Moss P and Pence A, 1999, *Beyond Quality in Early Childhood Education and Care*, Farmer Press, London and Philadelphia.

Heidemann S and Hewitt D, 1990, *Pathways to Play*, Redleaf Press, St Paul, Minnesota.

Kirkby M, 1989, 'Nature as Refuge in Children's Environments', *Children's Environments Quarterly*, Vol 6 No 1, pp 7–12.

Kylin M, 2003, 'Children's Dens', Children, *Youth and Environments*, Vol 13 No 1 Retrieved 12/04/07 from www.colorado.edu/journals/cye/13_1/index/htm.

Lazear D, 1999, *Eight Ways of Teaching*, Hawker Brownlow Education, Moorabbin Victoria.

Miller K, 1994, *Ages and Stages*, Telshare, Massachusetts, USA.

Rolfe S, 2000a, 'The Brain Research Phenomenon', *Every Child*, Vol 6 No 1 Australian Early Childhood Association, Canberra.

Rolfe S, 2000b, *Promoting Resilience in Children*, Australian Early Childhood Association, Canberra.

Standards and
stones

Barbara Champion

Introduction

This chapter considers the potential safety issues for early childhood educators working with children in natural outdoor playspaces. The information is based on the current Australian Playground Standards, however staff should also refer to local authorities to ensure the playspace meets all relevant local regulations and standards.

Importance of the natural environment as the basis for outdoor play

Young children need exposure to, and experience in, playspaces that provide learning opportunities in and about the natural environment. The constant change in natural playspaces as well as the complex variations of texture, sound and terrain, challenge children to approach each interaction with the natural playspace in new ways. Such interactions are fundamental to learning about resilience and risk taking, skills that cannot be acquired without on-going practice.

Children need outdoor playspaces that encourage some risk taking to promote self-managed behaviour. The benefits to children growing up in a natural play-space far outweigh any benefits from spending their early years in a structured, synthetic playspace, which does not allow for the seasonal changes, the manipulation of loose materials, and/or daily interaction with the natural elements. The generic synthetic playspaces do not promote the challenges and risk taking that the 'bubble wrap' generation of children so desperately need today.

Unfortunately, there is a common misconception that natural playspaces are more risky. Are they? Or is it just an over reaction to litigation concerns, a need for adult directed order and tidiness, or a sign of increasing 'generational amnesia' as discussed in the Introduction. Furedi (2001), a British sociologist, suggests that increasing concerns about risk and safety are part of a broader sociological trend in this generation and states in his article entitled 'Making Sense of Parental Paranoia':

> Apprehension about child safety, and a morbid expectation that something terrible can happen any moment, mean that many risks that are well worth taking because of their stimulating effect on a child's development are simply avoided. Child rearing today is not so much about managing the risks of everyday life, but avoiding them altogether (Furedi, 2001, p 19).

The following poem and illustration mocks some of these adult concerns about risk and safety (reprinted with permission).

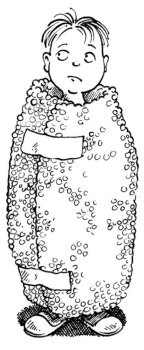

An example of the 'bubble wrap' generation.

I'm Lucky in Hurt Ways
I'm very lucky in getting hurt.
When I fell out of the peppercorn tree,
I fell onto the soft dirt.
Once, Faith accidentally kicked me in the head
(actually it was quite breathtaking;
she thought I was dead).
Her flying foot just missed my eye.
And when I broke my arm on the monkey bar,
an ambulance was passing by.

I'm lucky in hurt ways.
When I was going down and Emma was going up
on the trampoline,
my tooth went through my lip,
so her Grandpa bought us an ice-cream.
When I was little, I ran onto the road, and
a slow funeral car hit me.
And I was wearing my thick jumper
when the Schwartz's dog bit me.
(Honey, 1993, p 20–1)

A lucky fall!

However, safety is a major consideration when preparing for outdoor play in early childhood playspaces, including natural playspaces. Government authorities have requirements for funded services in particular and, as a rule, the Australian Playground Standards will apply. Relevant state government authorities can advise if there are particular requirements in a particular state or territory. Some States and Territories have produced their own outdoor play guides and these should be seen as a complement to Australian Playground Standards.

What are the Australian Playground Standards?

The Australian Playground Standards are guidelines developed on the basis of knowledge about injury and its causes. The Standards should be supported to ensure the safety of children in the outdoor play environment. There are three current key standards applicable to playgrounds and playspaces in Australia as listed below.

AS4685 2004 Playground Equipment

This Standard has the following Parts:
Part 1 General safety requirements and test methods
Part 2 Particular safety requirements and test methods for swings
Part 3 Particular safety requirements and test methods for slides
Part4 Particular safety requirements and test methods for runways
Part 5 Particular safety requirements and test methods for carousels
Part 6 Particular safety requirements and test methods for rocking equipment

AS/NZS 4422 1996 Playground Surfacing—Specifications, requirements
and test method, including amendment No. 1, 5th May 1999

AS/NZS 4486 1997 Playgrounds and Playground Equipment—Part 1
Development, installation, inspection, maintenance and operation.

It is sometimes thought that Australian Playground Standards require outdoor playspaces in early childhood centres to comprise manufactured items only, so as to conform to current Australian Playground Standards. This is definitely not the case.

Australian Playground Standards are largely about play equipment, its construction, installation and maintenance, and the ground surface. One of the benefits in using a natural playspace as the focus for children's play is that any anxiety about Australian Standards can be significantly reduced.

Natural playspaces are ideal for outdoor play, and as the Foreword to the Australian Standard on Playground Equipment AS4685 states:

> The primary aim of a playground should be to stimulate a child's imagination, provide excitement and adventure in safe surroundings, and allow scope for children to develop their own ideas of play. Ideally playgrounds should encourage development of motor skills and present users with manageable challenges to develop physical skills and to find and test their limits. In order to provide these challenges, a balance must be found between risk and safety. Professional advice should be sought, and children should be involved in planning, to ensure that the playground satisfies children's ideas of play and not those of adults (AS 4685, 2004, p 4).

What this highlights is the need for people working in the early childhood sector to understand the underlying approach and the key issues of the standards so as to put this knowledge into practice when working with children in a natural playspace.

Balance between risk and hazard

The Australian *Concise Oxford Dictionary* (Moore, 2003) describes a risk as 'a chance or possibility of danger' and a hazard as 'a source of danger or risk'.

Staff and management of children's services do have a great concern for the safety of children, however it is imperative that overemphasis on risk does not impact negatively on the appropriateness of the outdoor playspaces provided, or on outdoor play programs offered to children.

Also, children need to be able to make informed autonomous decisions about their own safety and to develop a positive self-image and competence in living skills. This is the concept of managed risk. They need opportunities to explore and experiment in a playspace that provides a degree of managed risk.

This chapter does not advocate that risk-free playspaces should, or could, be planned for children, but suggests strategies to develop quality outdoor playspaces, using the natural elements to the full, that will minimise avoidable injury.

In taking reasonable precautions to protect children from hazards, staff, playspace providers and management bodies need to make professional judgments about the likelihood of injury occurring and the severity of the injury. For example, a group of rocks located in a garden bed adjacent to an open area on which the children run, tackle and play ball games has the potential to cause injury, whereas a rock feature in a sandpit where play is more sedentary would not be considered a potential hazard given that it is not likely to cause an injury.

Key safety issues

The key safety issues to be understood by early childhood educators, playspace providers, management bodies and owners relate to:

- falling;
- collision; and
- entrapment.

Minimising injury from falling

When constructing playspaces, it is fundamental to ensure that young children are prevented from falling from heights that can cause serious injury, especially if falling onto a hard surface. The free height of fall, fall zone and ground surface are the main considerations to minimise injury from falling.

AS 4685 indicates that 1.5 m (1500 mm) is the maximum *free height of fall* (safe fall height) for supervised early childhood settings. However, it must be noted that the Playground and Recreation Association of Victoria (PRAV) states that this height is not applicable for children 0–3 years and recommends that a maximum of 1.0 m (1000 mm) is more appropriate for very young children.

A fall zone is required under and around any play item where the free height of fall is 500 mm or more from which a child could fall, so that the child's head in particular will not be injured. AS 4685 describes the fall zone as 'the surface that can be hit by a user falling from playground equipment'. It is the area under and around a piece of outdoor play equipment, where the free height of fall is 500 mm or more from which a child could fall (which includes a tree used for climbing, or any other natural material in the playspace), extending in every direction in which it is reasonably foreseeable that a child could fall. It is the minimum distance from any part of the play item to any hard surface, such as borders, paths, tree trunks, rocks, footings, obstacles or adjacent equipment.

The standard requires that the fall zone extend to a minimum of 1.5 m (1500 mm).

AS4685 stipulates that within supervised early childhood settings an increased fall zone is required where the free height of fall of the play item is greater than 500 mm up to a maximum height of 1500 mm. Where the free height of fall is

1.5 m (1500 mm) the fall zone must extend to a minimum of 1.9 m (1900 mm). This fall zone allows for the height of most young children and is measured from the item from which a child might fall plus any outward momentum they could have as they fall.

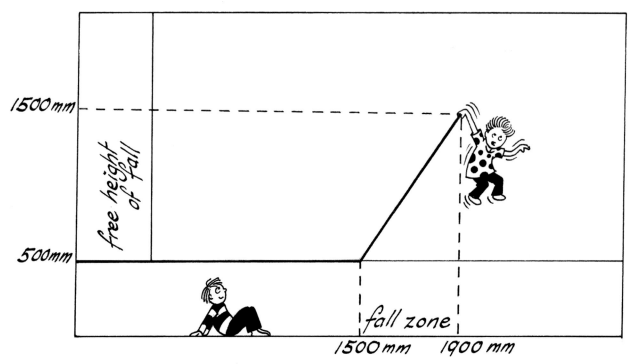

The relationship between the fall zone and free height of fall.

It is very important that natural playspaces have soft ground surfacing, when the potential to fall from any height above 500 mm exists. Impact absorbing surfaces are required in outdoor playspaces to reduce potential head injury to children as a result of normal play activity.

A significant body of scientific research indicates that the frequency and severity of playground injuries resulting from falls from playground equipment are substantially reduced where an *adequate impact absorbing surface* is provided.

AS/NZS4422 1996 Playground Surfacing states that an impact absorbing surface is needed wherever falls from play equipment, fixed or moveable, are possible —that is, in the 'fall zone'. Impact absorbing surfaces are required in any area under and around play items where falling is possible from a height of 500 mm or above.

PRAV advises that *there is a need for a wide variety of playing surfaces* to be available to children, and that every playspace should be assessed according to the needs of the children, the diversity of play experiences available to the children and the local availability of materials. There are many kinds of natural materials suitable for use as under surfacing including pea gravel, double milled woodchips, mulch, sand, pine bark, pea hulls and grass.

PRAV advises against the use of sand as a ground surface in Victoria and Tasmania, given the poor quality of sand available, however in large parts of Australia sand is the commonly used under surfacing material. Attention needs to be given to ensure that the sand provides appropriate impact absorption as required in AS/NZS4422. There are many kinds of sand and some sand can become as solid as concrete, which is therefore not suitable for under surfacing. Washed river sand and some beach sands are soft sand types and suitable. Also, some sand is of a granulated variety that does not absorb moisture, and thus does not compact, and is a good under surfacing material.

All loose materials need to be checked and/or turned over very regularly, depending on the use of the ground so as to maintain the impact absorbing qualities. A depth of 300 mm is recommended to be installed and maintained by regular checking against level indicator markings.

Further, we know that children sometimes fall when they are unable to gain support from use of their hands, and/or feet, so think about this when developing or using a natural playspace. A climbing structure, whether fixed or moveable, natural or synthetic, does need sufficient footholds and handholds to facilitate safe climbing.

Minimising injury from collision

Collisions can occur when children run into each other, or structures/natural elements in the outdoor playspace.

Sometimes the flow of children's movement around the playspace takes them across climbing or open ball game and running areas. This frequently causes collisions between children such as toddlers entering a boisterous ball game area, and collisions with climbing equipment such as when children chase each other through climbing areas.

The general layout of the playspace needs to be thought out so that there is a predictable and easy flow to the traffic of children moving in, and around the outdoor area. Outdoor play areas do not need to be full of equipment. In fact, a superior play area will be one which is regularly changing, and has plenty of space in which the children can create their own games and play. Supervision and the clear setting of behavioural limits are also important in minimising collision.

Minimising injury from entrapment

AS 4685 describes entrapment as a hazard in which a body or part of the body, or clothing can become trapped and the user is not able to break free and injury is caused by the entrapment. It is important to understand that it is only an entrapment when there is forced movement, and therefore the child cannot prevent becoming trapped, for example, when coming down a slide or a pole. An entrapment is not every gap or hole in the outdoor playspace where there is no forced movement.

Entrapment may occur via:

- whole body entrapment;
- head and neck entrapment;
- finger entrapment;
- foot and limb entrapment; and
- clothing entrapment.

It is important that adults supervising children in a natural playspace are always aware of potential entrapments. Frequently check trees, rocks and other natural items for potential entrapments. AS4685 should be referred to for entrapment measurement and testing details and/or support should be sought from PRAV or other advisory bodies.

Entrapment of a child's clothing could cause injury if it brings the child to an unexpected and abrupt stop. For example, a child coming down a slide, fire pole or tree may be stopped suddenly from descending further if cords, toggles or hoods from clothing become entrapped. Clothing cords and toggles can lodge in small gaps in sliding and other surfaces or wrap around protrusions. With the priority given to the wearing of children's hats for sun protection, it is recommended that hats with elasticised bands are preferable to any hat with a toggle or cord.

Specific safety issues to be aware of in natural playspaces

Every outdoor playspace is different, as is every child. Thus the importance is for staff, playspace providers and management bodies to understand specific safety issues, and their potential impact in the local environment:

- **Trip hazards** can be caused by uneven paving in pathways, intrusive tree roots in traffic areas or retaining edging can sometimes cause difficulties. For toddlers, trip hazards are a particular concern and must be avoided. Children need to experience differing surfaces and thus a diversity of surfaces is always recommended and children need to be shown the potential harm that some situations can create.

- **Rocks and hard edges** along pathways that may be used for running activities or around 'active' areas need extra care. Rather than remove items from the playspace, alert the children to the situation, and encourage caution on their part, or consider planted edges or borders that are softer and resilient.

- **Spreading sand onto paths** and other hard surfaces where it becomes a slip hazard can be avoided by regular maintenance by staff. Children can be also be encouraged to sweep sand, and/or a wider edge on sandpits may help to limit the spread. Toddlers are more prone to slipping on sand and extra care is needed.

- **Trees** play an important part in the natural playspace and should not be seen as a hazard without consideration as to their size, shape, sustainability, and general safety. The general rule of thumb is that if trees are part of a designated playspace for children, then extra care needs to be taken to ensure that they are in general good health, are not likely to lose branches, and are not a danger due to lack of maintenance. Children love to climb trees, and this is an excellent activity, but climbing heights and ground surfaces need to be considered if climbing is possible. When planning and designing outdoor playspaces, question the types of trees to be used, the free height of fall needed, the fall zone required, and the ground surfacing issues.

- **Sun protection.** The need for sun protection to reduce the risk of skin cancers is a critical health issue in Australia and elsewhere. In addition to personal sun protection practices in a centre, the incorporation of shade into the outdoor playspace design is essential.

Sun protection

Sun protection in early childhood reduces the risk of skin cancer. Children usually attend early childhood services in the hours of the day that have peak UV radiation risk, from 10 am–3.00 pm and this is frequently the time that children are outdoors.

Minimising the risk of UV radiation damage to young children, can be assisted by:

- *Designing outdoor playspaces to provide adequate natural shade;*
- *Organising programs to minimise the use of the outdoor play areas during daily and annual peak UV periods;*
- *Encouraging wearing of clothing that covers maximum amounts of the skin surface, sun protecting hats without cords and/or toggles, and sunglasses;*
- *Ensuring SPF30+ broad spectrum water resistant sunscreen is applied 20 minutes prior to any exposure and is reapplied after 2 hours;*
- *Staff and parents acting as role models in their use of appropriate clothing and skin protection; and*
- *Providing educative material about sun protection for children and parents.*

Sun protection is an ongoing responsibility for both staff and parents. Throughout Australia there are Cancer organisations with resources for the promotion of shade in outdoor play areas, and it is strongly recommended that contact be made with these agencies to receive appropriate information and support.

When planning and designing outdoor playspaces for sun protection consider:

- *the aesthetic and environmental advantages of natural shade, even if this means utilising temporary shade structures while waiting for vegetation to mature; how existing shade can be utilised by siting play areas directly under trees, near buildings or repositioning play structures; and*
- *indirect UV radiation from reflected surfaces such as concrete. Use shade to reduce reflective UV radiation. Also replace surfaces with less reflective materials such as brick, grass or mulch.*

Checklist for natural outdoor playspaces

When preparing for play in natural outdoor playspaces, give attention to:

- the entire site, and its current risks and potential risks and their solutions;
- feedback from families about the possible hazards for their children;
- location of play experiences in relation to the type of play area, for example, sandpit or climbing, to minimise the potential for intrusion and collision;
- changes in the natural environment which affect the playspace—organic changes or climatic conditions, for example, storm damage;
- bugs, spiders and other wildlife—what are the dangerous ones and what to do to minimise the risk, such as painting the inside of tyres white and ensuring planted tyres are filled to the top with soil to minimise spiders;
- water play—troughs, trickle streams, tanks, how to best use and manage these to conserve water and maintain safety; for example, avoid leaving water outdoors, incorporate a grate just under the surface of any ponds, ensure good drainage;

- bushy thickets or wilderness spots that create the illusion of seclusion and adventure for children, but supervision is required;
- ropes as moveable equipment—how long, how thick, what age group they are for, the type of setting and limits for their use by children;
- tyres for temporary gardens and edging—avoid steel belted tyres that may have protruding steel fragments;
- plants selected to ensure non-toxic and non-allergenic types;
- plants in babies' areas—check for loose parts that are too small that babies may mouth;
- logs have many uses—check for splinters, the type of wood, for example, slippery smooth bark when wet, and ease of movement; and
- rocks for edging and trickle streams or dry creek beds—check to ensure non-slip surfaces and ease of movement.

A final word on supervision

Supervision of children *in* the outdoor playspace is the most important ingredient in the provision of a safe play environment. All evidence to date indicates that when children are well supervised, that is, when adults are playing with the children, and/or are in close proximity, with a watchful eye on their movements, that the likelihood of injury is markedly reduced.

When planning supervision requirements consider:

- daily safety checks of the outdoor playspace;
- positioning of equipment, plants, rock areas and play experiences to facilitate supervision;
- adequate active supervision by staff including visual and or aural supervision and awareness of staff positioning in relation to the types of play experiences;
- children's skills, abilities, needs and current health in relation to the play experiences they are seeking;
- the importance of written policy and procedures about routines and practices to ensure consistency;
- the need to monitor the implementation of the policy and procedures;
- regular review of policies and procedures with all staff and parents involved with the children; and
- safety checklists to ensure that all staff have access to safety procedures within the service.

All children have the right to experience care and education in a healthy and safe environment. In developing systems to protect and maintain the well-being of all children and staff, management needs to consider safety in the context of the whole child. Safety considerations should be balanced appropriately with the individual and developmental needs of the child (Owens and Scott, 2004, p 7).

Conclusion

There is a greater need than ever before for children to play in natural outdoor playspaces.

Sometimes early childhood services can be intimidated by risk assessors who do not understand the early childhood sector and, in some cases, do not understand Australian Playground Standards themselves as pertaining to the Supervised Early Childhood Settings.

Early childhood educators and parents should persevere with efforts to develop natural playspaces and not be daunted by those who do not understand their importance. The benefits to children of a natural playspace far outweigh the safety concerns, especially given that safety is an issue for all kinds of playspaces and, thus, there is no evidence that a natural playspace is any less safe than a more conventional structured playground. Support is available to deal with any concern that may arise.

> Experience of nature is made possible as children are able to explore natural settings, their changes, smells, colours and feel; develop an appreciation of the natural environment; and begin to see their responsibility to foster and preserve this environment; and, provide memories of play in natural settings that will last a lifetime (Rogers, 2003, p 1).

> The spaces that teachers create for children seem to hold enduring memories for them that have a powerful influence on what they will value later in life (Fraser, 2000, p 53).

> *The best way to provide a safe outdoor play area is to provide a quality outdoor play program in a quality natural outdoor playspace.*

Resources

The Playgrounds and Recreation Association of Victoria

PRAV is an association whose membership comprises professionals, groups and individuals committed to promoting the value of play across Australia. They collect, disseminate and exchange information about play and play environments; encourage consultation with organisations and individuals on issues relating to play; facilitate research into the use of playgrounds and their value; promote better design of playgrounds; and encourage the better planning, design, development and maintenance of playspaces.

PRAV provides a telephone advisory service to the early childhood sector, schools, Local Government, State Government, playground manufacturers and community-based organisations on specialist aspects of planning, design, evaluation and development of play opportunities. They have a keen interest in policy development and research.

The PRAV website is an excellent resource and any early childhood service in Australia can become a member of PRAV to enable full access to the website support.

PRAV represents the play sector on the Australian Standards Committee and the Executive Director, Barbara Champion is the Chair of this Committee.

Ph 03 8846 4111
Fax 03 9846 7473
Email play@prav.asn.au
Website www.prav.asn.au

Kidsafe

Kidsafe NSW has a Playgrounds Advisory Unit that provides a regular newsletter 'Playground News' to NSW services and organises a biannual conference in NSW. Kidsafe New South Wales is located in the Children's Hospital at Westmead, Sydney.

Ph 02 9845 0890
Fax 02 9845 0895
Email kidsafe@chw.edu.au
Website www.kidsafensw.org

Environmental Solutions for Early Childhood Centres

There are two excellent booklets available to assist centres to deal better with environmental concerns:

- *Safer Solutions, Integrated Pest Management for Schools and Childcare Centres*; and
- *The Toxic Playground, a Guide to Reducing the Chemical Load in Schools and Childcare Centres*.

Both documents have been produced for the Total Environment Centre in Sydney and the contact details are as follows:

Ph 02 9299 5599
Fax 02 9299 4411
Email tec@tec.org.au
Website www.tec.org.au

References

Furedi F, 2001, 'Making Sense of Parental Paranoia', Retrieved 14/05/07 from http://www.frankfuredi.com/articles/parenting-20010425.shtml.

Fraser S, 2000, *Authentic Childhood. Experiencing Reggio Emilia in the Classroom*, Nelson, Ontario.

Honey E, 1993, *Honey Sandwich*, Allen and Unwin, St Leonards NSW.

Moore B, Ed, 2003, *The Australian Concise Oxford Dictionary 4th ed*, Oxford University Press, Australia.

Owens A and Scott C, 2004, 'Safety and Your Child Care Service', *NCAC Putting Children First*, Issue 12, pp 6–7.

Rogers K, 2003, 'Outdoor Play', Free Kindergarten Association, *Centre Spread Newsletter*, Winter Edition, pp 1.

Standards Australia International Ltd, 2004, *Australian Playground Standards AS4685 Playground Equipment. Standards* Australia International Ltd, Sydney.

Standards Australia International Ltd, 1996, *Australian Playground Standards AS/ NZS 4422 Playground Surfacing.* Standards Australia International Ltd, Sydney.

Standards Australia International Ltd, 1997, *Australian Playground Standards AS/NZS 4486 Playgrounds and Playground Equipment.* Standards Australia International Ltd, Sydney.

Bibliography

Tansey S, 2005, 'Supervision in children's services', *NCAC Putting Children First*. Issue 15, pp 8–11.

Making natural playspaces more accessible to children with
Disabilities

Mary Jeavons

Introduction

All children need to play, and children with a disability have exactly the same range of interests and needs as any other child or group of children.

Outdoors and natural settings offer open-ended play opportunities that are universally enjoyed by children, for many reasons and in many different ways. These settings may often be harder for children with a disability to engage with, as they may be physically less accessible, and require more intensive effort and intervention.

This chapter explores the elements of natural outdoor playspaces and investigates how these may be made more accessible to children with physical, sensory, cognitive and other disabilities.

Just like everyone else

A child with any kind of disability, whether mild or severe, is a child first and foremost. Children with disabilities want to play. They want to play with their friends and be part of the group. They want to fiddle with things, get there too, learn about their world, extend themselves, pretend stuff and muck around.

These children actually don't have special needs. They have exactly the same needs as everyone else. Too often it is easy to classify or label people with disabilities, so that we can think of them as different or 'the other'. This actually makes it easier to exclude them, if we don't consider them to be one of 'us'.

An underlying objective of this chapter is to help to revise this thinking. Children with disabilities are one of us. They are our child, our friend, our nephew or niece, or our brother or sister. They have abilities as well as disabilities. As we all do. They may need special assistance and support to have their needs met and for some children this may take a little longer.

Everyone likes a sandpit.

A simple change in thinking makes it a lot easier to include children with disabilities along with everyone else.

It is clear from the other chapters in this book that natural elements play a very important role in early childhood settings. Children with disabilities stand to benefit enormously from increased access to the natural world, and because that access may sometimes be limited, the value of early childhood centres with natural playspaces is magnified for these children.

Natural elements foster an understanding of the real ecological world. They provide settings of unique character, at a time in history when children are increasingly exposed to mass-produced products that are the same the whole world over. They stimulate imagination, creativity, engagement and intrigue, as they can be adapted for any purpose intended by the child. They provide beauty and constant change. They can be used in many ways.

Four roles for natural elements in early childhood settings

Some different roles for natural elements in early childhood centres are described below. The roles include: as a backdrop to define playspaces; to provide sensory experience of textures, scents, colours and forms; as tools for imaginative play; and simply for observation of natural processes.

The natural backdrop

Natural elements such as planting, boulders, logs, earthworks and land forming, can be used in a 'passive' role to *define* spaces which can be used for play and for other purposes, providing distinctive character and a child-like scale, creating hidey holes and cubby spaces, separating and protecting areas of different sizes, and providing a green backdrop.

Textures, scents, colours and forms

Textures, scents, colours, and forms *enhance* our physical world and add to the sensory richness of the outdoor environment.

Natural elements can be used to decorate, to add detail and character, and to reflect the local *character* of a place. These characteristics embed themselves into the psyche of a child and provide a sense of belonging to a particular land-scape. Dirt paths; seasonal flowers; the sound of frogs and local birdsong; pods to collect, rattle and sort; the smell of wet earth; shade and dappled light; and bright swathes of coloured flowers connect children to natural systems and provide meaning about their place in the world.

The tools for imaginative play, role-play and creativity

The *open-ended* forms of natural materials stimulate imaginative play as children work them into their own games. Every item has its own unique and distinctive character quite unlike anything mass-produced. As a manufacturer has assigned no purpose to it, children are able to adapt any object or material as required by their own imaginations. For example, a rock or low branching shrub may suggest a particular game and become the focus of activities in a particular space, and these activities will change as the children's interests change during the year.

Loose materials such as sand, dirt, pebbles, water, leaves, pods, twigs, flowers and grass clippings can be collected and frequently become the *currency* of play. They can be sorted and manipulated by children in their imaginative and creative activities and combined in countless ways to add to the *complexity* of play in other fixed parts of the playspace.

Natural process observation

Natural processes that take place (such as decomposition, food chains, growth, reproduction, weather and seasonal change) can be easily observed in a natural environment and are a rich source of education. The very presence of living plants, soil, water, grass, worm farms and compost demonstrate processes, life cycles and seasonal change while attracting creatures such as birds and invertebrate life that are a source of wonder and interest to all children.

All of these natural elements, used in any of the ways such as those described above, should be accessible to all children in all early childhood centres, but there are some specific challenges to be addressed to ensure both access and engagement for children with disabilities.

Attending early childhood services

During early childhood, children with disabilities may attend a mainstream kindergarten, preschool or child care centre, or they may participate in one of a range of specialised services such as early intervention centres depending upon the child's abilities and requirements. The attitude of staff, and their experience in working with children with disabilities, will have a significant impact on the play opportunities for a child with a disability.

Put simply, it is often difficult (especially in a big group) to provide the individual attention which the child with a disability may require to benefit from outdoor play alongside other children.

It is important to feel socially included.

To play with other children, and to play out of doors, may both be experiences that are challenging for children who may be slower than others, who may have more difficulty communicating, or who cannot physically reach the same playspaces as others.

An accessible and inclusive program that enables all children to participate fully will therefore need at least two components. One is social, and the other is physical. A physically accessible, appealing and intriguing outdoor space, with a good range of choices for play in nature, will make it much easier for staff and carers to assist the child with disabilities to play alongside other children out of doors. The body of this chapter will discuss *physical* solutions to making nature accessible. However, the social side is equally important and may in fact determine whether the child with disabilities ever reaches the outdoors.

Social inclusion is a precursor to accessing the great outdoors

For many parents coping with extra physical and emotional demands of caring for a child with a disability, kindergarten, pre-school or childcare can be confronting. Parents of a young child with a disability may not yet have acquired the necessary advocacy skills to ensure that their child's needs are met. Attending an early childhood centre may be one of the first times the parents and child have had to face physical and social exclusion. The parent will at times be dependent upon the assistance, goodwill and interest of the director, staff and other parents as well as specialists and therapists. Selecting the right centre will therefore be of utmost importance. A friendly and welcoming atmosphere and a willingness to explore and support a child's abilities will make a huge difference. Many staff will be concerned that they do not know how to help the child, and will possibly feel they do not have the additional staff or time required to provide the assistance that is required.

The type of disability varies widely, and a plan needs to be mapped out for each child to assist them to access play out of doors in the most effective way possible. Communication is essential. The director and staff need to learn about the child's interests and abilities and how to build on them, with the objective of including them in the most effective way. The best advice will usually come from the parents of the child, and from specialists such as paediatric occupational therapists, and speech and communication therapists, who can assist by providing advice, aids and solutions customised for each child.

Parents in turn need to learn how the staff work, what the program objectives are, and where their special understanding of their child will provide useful assistance to staff.

In particular, it will be important for the director of the centre to explain the benefits and objectives in terms of outside play and play in natural settings to parents of children with disabilities. Many children with frailties, illnesses, high support needs and limitations to their mobility have been highly protected all of their lives. It is possible that they have never played independently outside.

Abilities vary, but all can benefit from outdoor play.

Parents will be concerned about safety, infections and other risks. They may not understand what play in nature offers. It is important to separate out the 'real' concerns from the rest, and solve these so that children can reap the real benefits of a good outdoor play program.

At the beginning of the year, it is advisable for parents, staff and therapists to discuss the outdoor play program and work out together what steps will be taken to make sure that each child receives the assistance they need. Social inclusion requires good communication, co-operation and engagement, a willingness to be helpful, to try out solutions, and to make a child with a disability and their family feel that they are valued alongside everyone else.

Play outdoors and play with other children can be a real problem for many children with disabilities. Many simply do not have access to the same world that other children have. It is worth making the effort! The following practical points will assist directors, staff, management committees and designers to create inclusive accessible natural outdoor playspaces.

Implications of particular types of disabilities

Disabilities and their implications fall into a number of widely differing categories:

- intellectual, behavioural and cognitive disability;
- sensory impairments such as vision and hearing loss;
- long-term illnesses/organic conditions;
- physical disabilities which affect mobility, balance and/or ability to sit independently. These children may be only mildly affected (with perhaps poor balance), or may use a walking frame or sticks, or may use a wheelchair for some or all of the time; or
- a combination of the above disabilities.

The implications of any of these disabilities vary widely. They may obviously affect which parts of a playspace a child can reach and what they can do there. For some children, the outdoors may be physically difficult to reach without a path for their wheelchair or walking frame.

Some children may take a greater interest in particular aspects of the outdoors as either a direct result of their condition or to compensate for a loss. For example, children with vision impairments may take great pleasure and interest in the textures, auditory cues and sensory characteristics of their environment. Some children with autism can be absorbed in particular elements in space such as colours, lines or patterns, or perhaps spinning objects, and may also have a strong reaction against some aspect of a space such as particular sounds, colours, textures or smells.

Some very fragile or ill children will be unable to travel far before they need to rest, so easily accessible seating along easy paths will be beneficial. Also, back support on play equipment and seats will make it easier for children to sit or be supported. Shade will be important for many children, who may have heightened sensitivity to ultra violet (UV) radiation because of medication they take, or because of sensitive skin or eyes.

For children with vision impairment or a cognitive disability, a clearly legible path system that helps them to orient around a space will be a major benefit to independent play. A rail or other hand support may be helpful to both provide physical support and a guide around parts of a space.

Children can become absorbed in natural sensory elements.

The outdoor playspace can be designed with specific objectives that may have a 'therapeutic' outcome for particular children. While this is often an added benefit, it is worth remembering that play for play's sake is a vital part of children's development and anything that encourages play, fun and social interaction will by definition benefit the child. Therapy should not therefore be the only objective underlying an outdoor playspace.

Playing with soil.

Three universal ways to improve general access

Even though the implications of any disability will differ for every individual child, certain common solutions will make a big difference to the accessibility of most playspaces, and to natural spaces in particular. Three important ones include:

- seamless physical access into the natural playspace—path systems;
- front-on accessibility for wheelchairs; and
- seating for carers

Seamless physical access into the natural playspace—path systems

A path system makes a space accessible to children, with wheelchairs, walking aids or unsteady gait, which they otherwise may not be able to reach. An accessible route of travel needs to be gently graded with a firm even surface. Wheel stops, protective rails or hand support, may be required depending upon the function of the path (for example if it is for public access, or if there are falls off to the side), but smaller informal paths may not need these features. There are sometimes benefits in making the accessible path as narrow and informal as possible, as long as it is still functional, in order to remain at a child's scale and to avoid the appearance of a hospital corridor. A suite of Australian Standards address access and mobility, and these should be used as a guide. Relevant Australian Standards that may be useful for access to outdoor spaces are listed at the end of this chapter.

Mosaic patterns are absorbing elements for some children.

An informal and narrow, but accessible bush path.

Raised path edges are a helpful guide. When planting near paths, note thorny plants need to be treated with care. While it is important to avoid injuring children, encounters with the real world help educate children and expose them to the diversity of the plant world. There are many types of thorns—some are quite dangerous and others are simply a little unpleasant. Avoid planting thorny species where their thorns are a hazard, or where they catch clothing and form a nuisance, and where contact cannot be avoided.

Beware of paths that invite bikes and wheeled toys to make fast circuits through or around a space, these may place a fragile child at risk of being bowled over.

A legible path system or hierarchy of paths helps a child with intellectual disabilities to make sense of a space. The main path system can have smaller paths leading off into tiny areas, provide circuits and options in travel. A path is also an orientation guide for children with vision impairments. A raised, textured or contrasting coloured edge to the path will help them to orient themselves along it.

A handrail at child's height might be useful to support children with balance and mobility impairments and to help with orientation. Carefully placed rails can also double up as protection for garden beds and as balustrading where there is a change of level. A good design at the master planning stage integrates all of these elements into the overall design. The visual impact of 'special' features can be reduced to ensure that the space retains a friendly and non-institutional appearance while maximising the functionality of the space for anyone who uses it.

Choose *surfacing and materials* depending upon the purpose of the path:

- natural materials such as stone, paving or stepping stones in grass;
- compacted granitic gravel;
- coloured concrete, pattern pave or concrete with textures—exposed aggregate, mosaics, leaf textures and patterns inserted into the surface;
- stepping stones inserted into even common materials such as asphalt or concrete provide sensory interest and will assist a partly sighted child to find their way; or
- a path can deliberately provide bumps and texture for additional sensation, while wheeling especially.

This special creative feature is accessible from a range of levels.

< 116 >   The Outdoor Playspace Naturally

Stepping stone paths create a different tactile and visual experience and physical challenge.

A textured path provides additional sensory experience.

A path needs to be free of trip hazards and steps; needs to avoid very steep slopes; and should avoid soft, sandy or boggy patches. Prevent hazards such as overhanging branches and sections where a child could topple over an edge.

A path system will make it easier for all children to use small barrows and wheeled toys between spaces. It can usefully divide spaces from one another and will assist staff as they set up the playspace and move equipment from one area to the other. A useful, multi-purpose element, a path is nonetheless an expensive asset and needs to be very carefully placed within the space. It is important to avoid placing a path where it divides an otherwise useful space into two or more spaces that are then too small to be usable.

Front-on accessibility for wheelchairs

Many parts of a playspace require a child to be able to sit front-on to the activity. A child in a wheelchair will be unable to join in the play as successfully, unless there is knee-room underneath allowing them to sit comfortably face on. This is important for cubby shop counters, musical elements, interactive panels, water play and play at any kind of raised trough, raised sand, raised gardens and outdoor tables. An adjustable table that enables staff to set up play materials of any kind at the right height, so a child can sit or stand to reach or play, will be of great value. Make sure there is no obstruction underneath for knees. Suitable heights would be within the following range:

- clearance of between 575 mm and 640 mm from floor to underneath of the table/bench; and
- maximum overall height of between 715 mm to 780 mm (Standards Australia AS 1428.3-1992 Design for access and mobility—Requirements for children and adolescents with physical disabilities).

Please note that measurements vary widely and, where feasible, adjustable table or bench tops would be ideal. Recent (unofficial) measurements in a New South Wales program revealed a knee height on various children's wheelchairs ranging from 427 mm to 929 mm (Lovell, 2006). Also note, turning circles for wheelchairs vary depending upon the size and type of chair. A diameter range of around 1500 mm (small child) up to 2200 mm (adult) is required.

A wooden shop counter within this sculptured playspace allows wheelchair access.

Seating for carers

Many children with disabilities will need help and support to play. Extra perches in key areas such as at the sandpit, amongst some shrubs, in a cubby and near the digging patch will make it easier for carers to help a child. A seat with a back makes it easier to support a constantly moving child. A boat with a steering wheel would be fun for an adult and child to play together, but needs adequate room for knees, for both to fit, otherwise the experience is difficult and uncomfortable.

The general points above would each make a large difference to accessibility for many children in many settings. The next section describes in more detail some specific design elements to create inclusive natural playspaces for children with a disability.

Finding room to fit your knees in a boat can be challenging.

Extra perching places in and near the sandpit are useful for adults and children.

Access, inclusion and participation

The terms access, inclusion and participation are all slightly different. They are explained as follows:

- Access is a physical issue—whether someone can physically reach a space or an activity.
- Inclusion is more of a social issue, and requires an attitude that all children can take part in an activity, even if this requires some effort. Can a child be included in an activity? Do they feel part of the group? Can they sit together, fit at the table, fit in the cubby? It is hard to be included if you cannot physically access a space, so physical access is often a prerequisite for inclusion.
- Participation—once you can reach a space, and feel included if there are other people in the group, is there actually something meaningful you can do? Play a role in a game? Do the activity? Full participation usually requires both access and inclusion.

How to create inclusive natural playspaces with specific design elements

A range of specific design elements can be incorporated to promote an inclusive natural playspace from the choice of sensory-rich plants for pathway edging to calming retreats, accessible sand or water features and comfortable vantage points from which to observe nature. Thoughtful consideration of the range of possibilities is required.

The sensory qualities of plants and natural materials

The textures of plants and other natural materials provide a rich, sensory environment, which enhances all children's experiences of a space. For some children, texture is a particularly important way of receiving information, especially if their vision and/or hearing are limited. Ensure that interesting plants are within arms reach of a path or accessible seating area.

A calming environment

Every playspace needs some active areas and some quiet, more reflective places. The design of a space can suggest particular kinds of behaviour to children, and sometimes provides cues which are imperceptible to adults. Long, narrow spaces can inadvertently be perceived by children as 'runways' and cause frenetic activity that can be disruptive to other more sedentary activities. Similarly, some particular qualities in a space can suggest quiet, absorbing activities. The latter may function for a small group to play quietly and may provide an area where a frustrated or upset child may have time out with dignity.

Some design features of a calming accessible space might be:

- small size scale—a space between about 1800 mm and 2400 mm diameter is large enough for eye contact across the space for a small group, but does not permit any boisterous activities. Any larger and the small scale is lost;
- location away from a main running route or bike track and not used as a thoroughfare;
- partially enclosed with places to sit or lie, gaze at the sky, dream or rest;

Plants need to be accessible for close observation.

A small and calming space created with planting and seats.

- plant materials that are weepy, sensuous, soft and dark green or soft greys;
- quiet, or with subtle sounds, such as the sound of water, or wind in a copse of casuarinas; or
- an access route which a child with a walking frame or a child in a wheelchair can utilise.

Natural cubbies and small spaces

Some of the best cubby play occurs in places strongly defined by planting, with props adapted for the occasion enhancing the framework provided by nature. Where there are no (or very few) purpose-built elements, children's imaginative play creates a rich world, which in turn fosters communication, role-play and creativity. Children with disabilities may need assistance in getting into such spaces and in developing their role. This type of play is of just as much significance to them as to other children (and of possibly more importance, in helping them to overcome some of the effects of their disability), so any effort is well justified. Subtle intervention may be required by adults to help, but not take over.

An improvised cubby playspace created from a plank, tyres, logs and a pot plant. Items can be arranged and rearranged easily to suit particular accessibility needs.

Make such play more accessible with the following:

- plant groups of weeping type shrubs in a circle or semi circle and protect them while they grow;
- leave an opening wide enough for a wheelchair or walking aid and create a firm, but natural looking, wheelable surface;
- add a few bits of improvised furniture such as some low flat rocks, a box, blocks, or anything that can double up as seating for carers and for other children;
- use special features such as the hollow end of a log, a rock with a slight dish in it, a forked branch, or a plank with knot-holes to add sensory interest and a significant focus for the play;
- drape fabric over frames or branches to make the whole area into a 'new' space. Poles with hooks could be installed amongst the planting, for easy attachments;

- link such a space to the sand or digging patch to add another dimension. The sand will be carried between the two areas, so design it for easy sweeping and provide manageable carrying containers;
- encourage children to establish their own themes each day and to bring in the props they need—building, materials, cardboard boxes, a blanket, containers, etc. Every additional layer added to the space by the children increases the depth, complexity and longevity of the play;
- ensure that a child with a disability has access to some of the materials, can reach them, has their own special role and feels part of the game—perhaps a wheelchair tray or small accessible table will assist;
- create a shady green cubby with any kind of arbour frame or teepee and grow a fast growing climber, pumpkins or beans over it, improvised seating or supports for children and carers should be included too;
- plant a narrow tree 'tunnel' with close-spaced trunks and over-arching branches;
- grow corn plants and make a narrow path through them;
- investigate the British 'living willow' structures and adapt this idea into an Australian living cubby house. Australian plant species with the particular characteristics ('inosculate') that are required, include river red gums, and 'curtain figs' (Primack,1998). Many species of willows are unsuitable for use in many situations in Australia, as they are significant weed species; and
- ensure all the internal spaces are just wide enough for a wheelchair or walking frame and check the path and ground surface to maximise accessibility.

Creative play with loose open-ended natural materials

Creative and innovative planning can solve many access problems. The 'looseness' of many materials and natural objects provides automatic appeal for children, as objects in their own right, for their sensory qualities, and as a means to an end in their role-play and creative constructions. Children with disabilities, like everyone else, enjoy playing with materials such as sand and dirt, water, mud and clay, pebbles, shells, twigs, flowers, pods, leaves, and so on. Some ideas for using these materials and making them more accessible are:

- collect and manipulate them; and
- move them around.

Collect and manipulate them
A route through planting makes it easier to collect special seeds, flowers or leaves. Place them on a table or tray accessible to a leaning or standing frame, wheelchair etc. and provide a spot nearby for a carer to assist if required. Perhaps hang them in a net at grasping height for the child. Alternatively, provide trays, large bowls or troughs of pebbles, dirt, and autumn leaves or lawn clippings for sensory exploration.

Move them around
Adapt wheelbarrows, trays on wheelchairs, tricycles or simply pull along cardboard boxes to move loose materials. Provide a path system for children to take materials from one place to another. An outdoor area that has a range of smaller 'places' within it will be more interesting for children to move between the spaces. For example, two sandpits (one large, one possibly much smaller) sets up a connection for movement between the two. Young children enjoy barrowing sand, leaves, pinecones etc, from one place to the other. A child with physical disabilities may be able to use a tricycle with a trailer; their wheelchair may be able to help 'carry' things. Barrows that can be easily pulled or pushed while providing balance and support will also help a disabled child join in.

A tray is useful for collecting and carrying natural treasures.

Sand

Sand has endless possibilities as a play medium. A good working surface is important. This can be something moveable—a small table, plank, box or cable reel—or can be fixed—a wide timber edge, some wide flat boulders, or a raised fixed table edge.

Sand works well if associated with some 'cubby'-like elements. It is also ideal to have planting nearby, especially durable planting which can supply constant flowers and leaves for play in the sand.

Sand is always improved by the addition of water. Wet sand is malleable and the possibilities of directing water, channelling it and directing its flow are endless.

Sand is ideally located away from buildings and off main public access pathways. It is generally better to locate the sand *below* the surrounding levels to limit spillage, and to provide a sloping beach-like, sweeping edge along the main entry (rather than a raised edge) which allows sand to be swept back into the pit.

For children with physical disabilities, access to sand needs to be considered. A multitude of access solutions may be suitable, depending upon the physical and social needs of the child.

Access issues could include:

- Physically getting into the sandpit or digging patch. A sloping beached edge will be easy for a child who can crawl. A raised edge may be used as a transfer station from a wheelchair. A simple rail or handgrip may help children with poor balance get themselves into the sand.
- Provision of support while sitting or lying in sand. Something to lean against for either the child or carer will be of assistance. A leaning 'wedge' might allow a child to lie in the sand, raising their trunk sufficiently so they can play in the sand with arms and hands.
- A wheelchair accessible raised sand table on the edge of the sandpit will provide sand play for children in wheelchairs. As for play tables, suitable heights are difficult to determine because of the range of types of chairs, but would be within the following range—

  - clearance of between 430 mm and 700 mm from floor to underneath of the table/bench (check the heights suitable for the children attending); and
  - maximum overall height of between 715 mm to 780 mm (AS 1428.3-1992 Design for access and mobility—Requirements for children and adolescents with physical disabilities);
  - depth (that is, from front to back, measured horizontally) should be between 300 mm and 650 mm clear space, to fit knees and feet under).

A leaning wedge in the sandpit promotes access.

- Structurally connecting the sand table to the rest of the sandpit will link the two and make it more likely that the children will play together. Pouring equipment, funnels and scoops and lengths of pipe and tubing will encourage interactive play.
- Relocateable mats over sand can allow a child to wheel into the sand (see 'Mobi mats', Deschamps (2005).
- A hammock over the sand may allow a child to take part in some way, or simply to be there while other children play in the sand.

A timber bench in the foreground facilitates engagement with the sand area, providing a working surface where children can build and pour, and work with other materials.

Safety issues and sand

- *Take care with sand in bearings and fittings on wheelchairs and walkers.*
- *Sand spilt onto paths can be a slip hazard.*
- *Sand can irritate sensitive skin, and some children who are touch-sensitive may detest the sensation of sand.*
- *Dry sand can be very glary and has a very high reflective index that means ultraviolet radiation is easily reflected. Shade over the whole sand play area is therefore very important as children with limited mobility can spend a long time in the one position.*

Water

There are endless ways of enjoying water play for all children, regardless of abilities. Water can be calming, provides sensory and auditory stimulation, and can be combined with other materials (sand, dirt, soap, bubbles, and so on) to stimulate exploration, creativity and imaginative play for children who may be less able to engage with more physical activities in the playspace. It is also a medium which attracts other children to play together, stimulating communication and social interaction. A water feature such as a small fountain could be used as a focal point which encourages children to explore and move around a space. Other ideas include:

■ Moveable troughs that can be used in a standing position or accessed from a wheelchair are possibly the simplest. Aqua play (AquaPlay AB, 2006) is a flexible toy/product with many possibilities for setting up on a table or floor.
■ A water wall, accessible to children standing, or in wheelchairs or with walking aids, where water flows over a wire mesh screen into a channel of varying heights along which children can dabble and float things
■ A hose filled stream flowing into a sandpit or digging patch. This may have raised sections that can be accessed from a wheelchair or used standing up, though there can be difficulties in preventing climbing on such raised sections.
■ Water in combination with sand or dirt, rocks, planks, logs and other building materials encourages serious dam and channel construction. This in turn requires communication, co-operation and many other skills. A multi-level sand play area, with a water source at the top, may facilitate a child to play from a wheelchair or walking aid at the raised end. Intensive supervision will be required if spades and other digging equipment are used.

A creative water wall provides an engaging sensory experience.

This raised, hollowed-out log at Perth Zoo can be used as an aqueduct and filled from a hose (drought permitting) and the water can flow into the sand, dirt or a garden. The height of the log can be set so it is easily accessible and the ground surface can be paved or rubberised for easy access. Climbing on the log needs to be managed to prevent injuries from falls.

■ Small mucky areas with tough planting, rocks, and water on demand, can be created in permanent zones in the playspace, but these can also be created for temporary use in raised troughs or at tables where a child requiring physical support can reach them. Seasonal materials can be brought in.

■ Water in the form of a frog pond or bog environment (fenced off if necessary), though not really a play setting, is valuable for nature observations and to provide visual amenity, even if this can only be enjoyed in a passive way.

Productive gardening

Most children enjoy gardening, especially if they can grow and eat produce from their own garden. The whole process of digging and gardening is an extended sensory and learning process which could start with researching the right plants to grow, preparing the soil, digging and planting, watering, weeding and observing the plants growing and flowering. Then there is the excitement of harvesting, cooking and eating. The pleasures of monitoring the life cycles of attendant bugs and the fun of researching how to prepare the fruits or vegetables can culminate in the social and cultural celebrations of the food, and enjoying eating together. Children with disabilities enjoy every part of this project alongside everyone else.

■ Raised beds might help to prevent children running across the garden, which in any case need to be carefully located out of traffic routes. A raised garden bed will need an overhang of between 430 mm and 700 mm if it is to be accessible from a wheelchair.

■ Terracotta strawberry pots or other pot designs with vertical pockets from which the plants spill out will make access from a variety of angles possible.

■ Teepees and arbours that support climbing plants might invite a child in a wheelchair to pick fruits and vegetables while enjoying the temporary green cubby inside.

■ Hay bales make relevant propping places for children and carers.

■ Accessible gardening tools appropriate to the skills of the gardeners are essential.

■ Potatoes grown in tyre stacks are an easy crop to harvest and the stack itself is a supportive prop for close observation of potato plant growth.

These raised gardens at the Ian Potter Foundation Children's Garden, Royal Botanic Gardens Melbourne allow young children to stand at the edges to garden.

Raised garden beds at various heights and with appropriate overhang facilitate access.

Digging in the ground with your hands for potatoes can be a challenging experience with edible rewards.

Places to observe nature

A space with vegetation which attracts local wild birds and provides habitat for lizards, butterflies, insects and other invertebrates invites the incidental interest of children. This may be especially significant for the child who cannot be as physically active and who may spend a lot of time observing their surroundings or perceiving sounds, textures, colours or smells.

A quiet, accessible space, protected from busy activities, and possibly surrounded by suitable plants with seasonal flowers will encourage wildlife. Sometimes such an observation area can be located where children can look out over tree tops (such as at the top of a slope, or from a verandah or balcony) and see birds and flowers on treetops close by. A carefully placed nesting box or birdbath may prompt interest and observation.

If domestic animals can be properly cared for, a small enclosure such as an aviary or a fish tank can similarly provide many benefits for children. If children are able to get inside the enclosure, make sure that the gate is wide enough for a wheelchair or walking aid and there is an accessible route inside. Where children observe from outside a fence, ensure that the top rail of the fence does not block the view of a child in a wheelchair or using a walking aid.

In conclusion

Accessibility is often determined as much by social inclusion and resourcefulness as by physical design. The attitudes of staff and management will be vital in determining whether a child with a disability feels included in any service and especially in the outdoor program. Staff need to be conscious of the importance of outdoor play, and the value of nature and natural elements. Natural elements in an early childhood centre do not need to be on a grand scale. They can be quite small, but will make a big difference.

The timber enclosure on the raised platform is an ideal bird hide for observation. It also provides a range of sensory experiences including a feeling of enclosure and engaging patterns of shade and light.

With some forethought, and careful design, it is possible to make a much wider range of natural settings and materials more accessible to children with disabilities. A combination of:

- accessible, flexible designs, that can be adjusted as required; coupled with
- staff who can imaginatively adapt situations so that all children can participate, will assist children with disabilities to become more active participants in their own play in natural settings.

Acknowledgments

Photos were taken in the following places. The chapter author would like to thank these centres, schools, councils and individuals.

Aurora School, Blackburn
Belmore Special School
Central Carlton Children's Centre
City of Albury Patricia Gould Reserve
City of Port Phillip—Alma Park
Croydon Special School
East Melbourne Child Care Cooperative (Berry St)
Harry and Rhoda Jeavons
Harry Jeavons Jnr and family
Norparrin Early Intervention Centre, Mill Park
Nepean Special School, Frankston
Royal Botanic Gardens, Melbourne
Perth Zoo Play Space

References

AquaPlay AB, 2006, *Aqua Play* Retrieved 10/4/07 from http://www.aquaplay.se/canalsystems.html.

Deschamps, 2005, *Mobi Mats Deschamps* Retrieved 10/4/07 from http://www.mobi-mat-deschamps.com/.

Lovell G, 2006, Personal communication.

Primack M, 1998, *The NSW Good Wood Guide* —PLEACHING Rainforest Information Centre Retrieved 10/10/06 from http://www.rainforestinfo.org.au/good_wood/pleachng.htm.

Bibliography

Christensen KM, *Creating inclusive outdoor play environments Designing for ability rather than disability* Retrieved 10/10/06 from http://www.adventureislandplayground.org/Keith%20Christensen%20article.PDF.

Department for Victorian Communities, 2007, *Good Play Space Guide: 'I can play too'*, Department for Victorian Communities, Melbourne.

North Carolina State, *University Natural Learning Initiative* Retrieved 10/10/06 from http://www.naturalearning.org/.

North Carolina State University Co-operative Extension, *Making the Most of Outdoor Time with Preschool Children* Retrieved 10/10/06 from http://www.ces.ncsu.edu/depts/fcs/human/pubs/FCS507.pdf.

Australian Standards relevant to outdoor access

AS 1428 (Set)—2003: *Design for access and mobility*

Includes the following in the set:

- AS 1428.1—2001 *Design for access and mobility—General requirements for access – New building work*
- AS 1428.2—1992 *Design for access and mobility—Enhanced and additional requirements—Buildings and facilities*
- AS 1428.3—1992 *Design for access and mobility—Requirements for children and adolescents with physical disabilities*
- AS/NZS 1428.4—2002 *Design for access and mobility—Tactile indicators*
- AS 1428.7—Outdoor access (in progress)

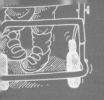

Planning for children in natural
playspaces

7

Michelle Hocking

Introduction

A natural playspace dominated by plants and incorporating a number of smaller defined areas or features is a fertile environment in which to plan and implement an early childhood program. The purpose of this chapter is to give the reader an understanding of the potential of a natural outdoor playspace for children's engagement and learning. Specifically, theoretical perspectives that underpin approaches to planning early childhood curricula, how a natural playspace supports opportunities for play, and some practical considerations when planning and creating play experiences in natural playspaces.

This chapter is not intended to be prescriptive in terms of an actual program planning format. There is no one definitive format and staff usually select one which best suits the needs of each centre, influenced by previous practices at the centre, current ideology, staff experience, centre policies and practicalities such as sharing of the playspace.

Theoretical perspectives that underpin approaches to planning

With the revisiting and reassessment of Developmentally Appropriate Practice (DAP) (Fleer, 1995; Fleer and Richardson, 2004) as a planning 'template' and the emergence of alternative rationales for planning and curriculum design, early childhood educators may find themselves bewildered and even threatened by the varied alternative 'templates'.

There are many perspectives that guide current thinking, and the exciting thing is we don't have to 'throw the baby out with the bath water'. Although we are, and will continue to be challenged to change and modify our practice, these alternative options for curriculum also reinforce much of our philosophy, validate our own current practice and give us permission to engage in a little risk taking of our own when planning programs.

Some perspectives to consider

Some perspectives to be considered in planning include:

- sociocultural perspective;
- Reggio Emilia approach;
- infant brain development;
- multiple intelligences; and
- Steiner philosophy.

The sociocultural perspective

The sociocultural perspective challenges us to look more deeply into the impact of life experiences, ethnicity, values, gender and environment on the young child and stresses the importance of developing a well rounded knowledge of each individual child that includes family values and beliefs. Consider how the philosophies underlying a natural playspace reflect the values of the families in the following two anecdotes.

> *I received a phone call from a woman who was pregnant with her first child. She rang Environmental Education in Early Childhood Vic Inc (EEEC) looking for the names of early childhood centres in her area that were compatible with her*

environmental values. She had been to visit several centres but was concerned that their outdoor playspaces featured 'fake grass and plastic toys'. She emphasised that this was not what she was looking for in an early childhood service for her child.

I was able to pass on to her the names of several long day care centres and kindergartens in her area that had natural playspaces and incorporated natural materials into their programs as part of an holistic approach to early childhood environmental education.

(Source: Archives of Environmental Education in Early Childhood Vic. Inc., 2003)

Upon first viewing the natural outdoor playspace a prospective parent was overheard to comment 'When I saw the playground I knew this was the centre for my child'.

(Source: staff member, Coburg Children's Centre Melbourne)

The Reggio Emilia approach

The Reggio Emilia approach describes teaching strategies as 'scaffolding' or 'guided participation' requiring children to have the support and guidance of more skilled adults and peers in an apprenticeship approach to learning. Rogoff (1990) highlights children's needs to observe and participate with these more skilled others in order to build on their knowledge and construct new solutions and to have time for the processes of observing, practising and gaining competence through experimentation and repetition. The programs of Reggio Emilia and the theories of Vygotsky suggest learning is different from development. A scaffolded learning approach stresses the importance of interactions with peers, validates the use of small groups, interest-based projects and complex play requiring verbal interactions.

Embedded in this approach is the notion of the environment as a teacher. There is less emphasis on changing the environment and more on adding open-ended materials and resources to interest areas. An aesthetically pleasing environment is fundamental to this approach. In a natural outdoor playspace, an environmentally aware and sensitive adult has endless opportunities to use techniques such as modelling, describing, questioning, suggesting and recalling for scaffolding children's learning.

For example the adult who:

- sits on the grass with a baby rather than find a blanket, and play peek-a-boo;
- might exclaim their delight in the beauty of a fragrant flower, takes the time to stop and smell it, then might bring out a magnifying glass to take a closer look;
- discusses the dilemma of 'do we leave flowers on the bushes to grow or is it OK to pick them?' ; or
- reminds children of the time they grew climbing beans on a tripod of stakes and recalls these skills to assist with building a cubby from bamboo lengths.

Infant brain development

Current discussion of research into infant brain development indicates the importance of quality, interactive nurturing in the early years (Corrie 2000 cited in Arthur, Beecher, Death, Dockett and Farmer, 2005). Nurturing includes behaviours and aspects of the environment which support the child's emotional well-being; such as comforting physical contacts or verbal exchanges that are mutually satisfying and consideration of the aesthetics of the play setting.

Such nurturing builds self-esteem and positively reinforces individuality that is foundational in goal setting with young children. In a natural outdoor playspace there are many opportunities for such interactions.

For example:

- a reading area, made from soft cushions in subtle tones, underneath the shade of mature tree ferns; or
- in a quiet corner, two doll hammocks improvised from 'orange bags' and dowel lengths are suspended between trees, two baskets of doll clothes are placed on log rounds, two wooden prams are parked nearby.

Multiple intelligences

Gardner's Multiple Intelligence's reinforces the importance of planning for the 'whole child'. Each of the intelligence's: logico-mathematical, linguistic, spatial, musical, bodily-kinesthetic, naturalistic, existential, intrapersonal and interpersonal (Gardner, 1983; 1999) reflects a different ability, such as the ability to reason and think logically or the ability to understand the feelings of others. A program that provides for a variety of experiences maximises opportunities for each child to access and display their different domains of intelligence. A child who draws a plan for their cubby construction is exploring a different domain of intelligence than a child who can work out how to dam the flow of a watercourse. Naturalistic intelligence relates to children's perceptions of and relationship with the natural environment. A child with naturalistic intelligence would recognise members or elements of a class of natural objects. This child might sort a collection of rocks, readily observe different bird types or select a particular type of leaf to mix into sand 'stew'. Beyond direct observation and manipulation, such a child might demonstrate caring attitudes towards plants and animals and share a particular sense of wonder and enthusiasm in relating to the natural environment.

Steiner philosophy

The Steiner philosophy of education is an approach where the consideration of the emotional, physical and spiritual aspects of a child's being is fundamental. A setting where 'the child is allowed to take in the world through his senses and to participate in it through movement, making things, and play' (Baldwin Dancy, 2000, p 294). In recent years there appears to have been an increasing interest in this philosophy by more mainstream educators. Schools are offering Steiner streams and many early childhood staff source imaginative play and nature-based reference materials from Steiner play equipment suppliers. In a Steiner setting, children play freely for long periods of uninterrupted time, but come together for snacks or meals, circle time and story times. Thus, each day has a strong sense of rhythm. Seasonal change is celebrated during festivals involving all family members. Imaginative play materials are hand-carved, collected with care or sewn lovingly in the presence of children. Steiner environments are aesthetically beautiful, indoors and out. Consider how expressions of joy, contentment, enthusiasm and a sense of achievement are manifested in these settings and others where natural outdoor playspaces are the backdrop for children's play.

Program planning as a landscape painting: four layers of complexity

When program planning for a natural outdoor playspace, it is useful to reflect on four layers of complexity that the landscape provides as the setting for play, just as one might reflect on an oil landscape painting. These four layers are:

1. the playspace as a whole;
2. defined smaller areas;
3. loose materials and equipment; and
4. prevailing and seasonal weather conditions.

The four layers are somewhat analogous to creating an oil painting with multiple layers of paint, each layer of paint adding complexity and depth and each contributing to the whole landscape. In reality not all early childhood outdoor playspaces offer the four layers of complexity to the same degree and, unfortunately, many early childhood educators will be working in centres where this is far from the current situation. For centres where these natural layers of complexity are lacking, this chapter includes practical ways that some natural playspaces can be improvised.

Layer 1

Layer 1 is the *playspace as a whole*, the overall aesthetic impression that is gained from the first viewing. First impressions are often visual and, in a natural playspace, might include the amount and diversity of vegetation, the variation of ground surfaces, access to areas via pathways and specific features such as a trickle stream, digging patch or water tank. This provides the backdrop for children's play, but is not a backdrop in a static sense. It is dynamic and as such impacts on program planning and children's play.

Layer 1 The playspace as a whole.

Layer 2

Well designed natural playspaces provide a range of *defined smaller areas* variously referred to as enclosed spaces, dens, garden rooms or habitats within the overall space. Within a natural setting the 'plant-scape' can and should be used to help define the smaller playspaces. Crook and Farmer (2002, p 18) refer to the use of 'bushy parts of the playground' as one method for defining playspaces with minimal distractions, 'increasing the likelihood of productive play and a high level of concentration'.

Also, there are specific features such as trickle streams, gravel pits and vegetable gardens as described in Chapter 3. These *defined smaller areas* provide foci for planning specific experiences.

Layer 3

The third layer is the *loose materials and equipment* that an adult or child might add to these spaces to constitute the planned and spontaneous play experiences that are the 'nuts and bolts' of the early childhood program. Natural loose materials are abundant in natural playspaces and the types of equipment required will reflect the play experiences likely in such a playspace; for example, spades for digging, rakes for gathering leaves, baskets for collecting seed pods, wheelbarrows/trolleys for carting small logs, watering cans for gardening. Also, open-ended waste materials such as tyres, reels and wooden off-cuts support a consistency of approach to creating play opportunities.

Layer 2 a small enclosed playspace
'secret garden' with Layer 3 loose
materials for dramatic play at
The Lady Gowrie Child Centre,
Melbourne.

Layer 4

The fourth layer is the *prevailing and seasonal weather conditions*. Imagine looking out into a playspace and being able to add another dimension to the program simply by responding to the weather conditions on any given day and to the predictable seasonal changes throughout the year. In a natural playspace these conditions can be the stimulus for a variety of learning experiences that connect children directly with the natural world. A natural playspace reflects what is happening in the elements; branches, webs and play cloths move with the wind, balls of water collect on nasturtium leaves after rain, puddles evaporate when the sun shines. How many of these moments can be captured in a play-space dominated by artificial surfaces, fixed structures and minimal vegetation?

The 'secret garden' once shaded by the wattle tree will take time to re-establish. Natural brush was secured to the exposed wall, a teepee now provides shade and a new tree has been planted.

Realising the potential of natural outdoor playspaces for program planning

A natural outdoor playspace is a constant yet ever-changing environment. If playspaces are intended to attract, engage and delight children, then a natural outdoor playspace meets all these criteria and more. When considering the potential of any natural playspace it is a useful exercise to ask yourself the following questions.

1. What might children do in this space as it is?
2. What loose materials or props might be added to the space to enhance and challenge the child's knowledge and/or skills?
3. What might be the adult's role in this situation?

Of course the answer to what children 'might' do in a space may be quite different to the play that emerges. The child's age and level of development, particular interests, well-being on a particular day or prior exposure to similar environments are all influencing factors. Nevertheless, it is useful to ponder the possibilities both at the planning and design stage of the playspace and during program planning time to ensure that there is always a range of experiences available at any given time.

The potential of a natural outdoor playspace for program planning can also be explored through the four layers of complexity previously described. Consider the example of a water tank initially as a fixed feature of the outdoor playspace. Practically speaking it is a receptacle for the collection of rain water (layers 1 or 2). Then, think about the number and variety of experiences that might develop with the addition of loose materials and props (layer 3) and in response to particular weather conditions (layer 4). For example:

■ measuring and documenting the amount of rain that has collected in the tank—During periods of rain, buckets and other containers might be placed outside for additional collection. In this way, the amount that has fallen can be 'seen'. A rain gauge or clear Perspex measuring pipe on the outside of the water tank would also assist in this process;

■ adding 'junk' containers for transferring tank water such as plastic bottles, tin cans, ice-cream containers, plastic honey buckets, empty pump bottles, milk cartons etc;

■ gardening with herbs such as mint that thrives in areas where it might get additional water, it also gives off a lovely fragrance as children brush past to get to the water tank tap and could be used in real or pretend cooking experiences;

■ listening to the sound the rain makes as it enters the tank from the guttering and imitating this sound using percussion instruments as part of a music experience; or

■ discussions about water as a precious resource, that it can 'run out' and linking this with other water conservation practices in the centre.

The potential for child initiated discovery to provoke program planning is vitally evident in natural outdoor playspaces. Staff responsive to this provocation will find many learning opportunities to explore with children. Discoveries waiting to be made in natural outdoor playspaces might include:

■ rocks in the shade feel cold and in the sun feel warm;
■ insects, bugs and beetles crawl out and scatter away from rolled over logs (be vigilant but positive should spiders crawl out!);

- some leaves stay green all the year and others change colour and fall to the ground;
- buds change into flowers then edible seed pods;
- leaves can be shiny, furry, smooth, pliable, pointed or crinkled;
- seeds with wings or burrs and seeds that just grow everywhere;
- seed pods can rattle, 'explode' or float;
- bark can be long and stringy, smooth or knotty;
- large rocks are heavier and harder to move than small ones;
- spiders use plants to attach their webs;
- when clouds move across the sun one cannot make shadows;
- worms burrow away from sunlight;
- if you hide behind a bush it is harder to be seen by other people; or
- tomatoes that you grow yourself taste fantastic.

The potential to develop further play experiences and learning opportunities from this list of observations and discoveries is unlimited. Each will be enhanced and extended with the interactions of a supportive adult and additional prop materials. Create your own list based on observations of the children in your centre and use it to stimulate ideas for planned play experiences. Beyond the physical playspace, prevailing weather conditions may inspire a variety of spontaneous responses that become part of the program. For example:

- simply watching the rain drops slide down windows;
- splashing in puddles wearing wet weather gear;
- making boats to float in the puddles;
- drawing a line around a puddle at intervals to measure the rate of evaporation
- measuring and documenting the rainfall using a rain gauge over a day, week, month or year; or
- constructing kites or wind chimes on windy days.

Also, seasonal changes and conditions are more likely to be noticed in natural playspaces and can be extended upon. For example:

- knowing the right season to plant tomatoes/corn/peas/beans;
- identifying the time of year to wear hats and sunscreen and play under shady trees;
- observing the birds that feed on native blossom at particular times of year;
- finding cicada nymph shells on tree trunks in summer;
- noticing that after the bare branches of winter comes the blossom on the fruit trees in spring; or
- watching sunflowers follow the sun in summer.

Natural playspaces also have an aura of authenticity. In keeping with this aura they are most suited to the addition of real props such as garden tools, wheelbarrows, metal spades, pulleys, woodworking tools, pipes or timber off-cuts. The value of children engaging in 'real' work has been previously reported by Lunt and Williamson (1999) and is discussed in Chapter 4 in relation to child development. Program plans incorporating real work opportunities can also support the creation of new areas in the playspace such as fairy or dinosaur garden type ferneries, frog ponds and herb gardens.

From the staff perspective, when program planning for a structured outdoor playspace adults need to be prepared to move equipment and set play props to provide many of the experiences. For example, an indoor table is moved outside with a large coloured plastic tray and multi-coloured sand toys for imaginative sensory play. In contrast, in a natural playspace an adult may simply place some spoons and old pots under a tree near mulch or leaf litter and a

sensory experience is created without significant movement of equipment. As the play materials blend with the natural environment they are not so obvious as to distract children, but can be simply 'discovered' as children walk past. In addition, should children require further props to extend the play such as water, tree trunks sections, tyres, rocks or gum nuts, these are readily at hand in a natural playspace. A natural playspace requires minimal setting up of equipment as the space itself is conducive to so many discoveries and play opportunities.

Planning play experiences

When planning and creating the play experiences within a natural playspace there are a number of questions to consider and some of these are discussed below.

1. How many children will be using the playspace at any given time throughout the day/session?

This will impact on the number of specific places for play to be provided. A natural playspace has the potential to provide more specific playspaces than a structured playspace and even the small and shrubby corners invite one or two children. Crook and Farmer (2002, p 38) state that 'generally speaking there needs to be between five to ten more playspaces available than the number of children in the group'. For example, if a group of 20 children is planned for, there needs to be 25–30 specific playspaces available. Using this simple practical formula as a guide, staff can easily determine (by a head count and visual survey of the area) whether there are enough specific playspaces at any given time for the number of children and adjustments can be made accordingly.

The 'five to ten more playspaces' formula allows for the following options to be available to the children within the space:

- move from one specific playspace to another different one;
- move in and out of the same specific playspace; or
- remain for a period of sustained play without feeling pressured (by staff or other children) to 'give someone else a turn'.

That children within a group will engage in a range of solitary, parallel and co-operative play situations throughout a session/day is also supported by ensuring there are more specific playspaces than the number of children in the group.

In order for staff to ensure sufficient playspaces for the number of children, written program plans could indicate the number of children staff anticipate can be accommodated comfortably at each play experience. The following example from a program plan indicates how this might be achieved if planning for four children at a sand mark making experience:

> *Sand mark making experience—4 wooden sand trays on circle of log rounds, basket of dowel lengths for mark making and sand smoothers, X 4 children*

The number of children that the specific playspace has been prepared for might be quite different to what eventuates in practice. It might be that only one or two children at any given time are involved in the mark making experience. Staff might choose to leave it prepared for four children or modify the experience, so instead of four log rounds in a circle, two log rounds up against a fence, wall or hedge might be a better use of the space. This change results in a reduction by two in the number of specific playspaces available. Written plans might incorporate this modification to ensure the overall 'five to ten more spaces' formula is maintained. Some early childhood educators may prefer to be less prescriptive and more reflective about the number of playspaces, however understanding of the relationship between places to play and the number of children is essential even if not documented.

2. Does the playspace invite manipulability?

It is not just the number of specific playspaces, but the potential for manipulability of the whole playspace that will have a significant impact on the dynamics of the playspace at any given time.

Kritchevsky and Prescott's (1977) work on analysing playspace developed in the 1960s and 1970s is still a useful guide to assessing the potential extent of children's constructive participation in a particular setting. Playspaces are characterised as either 'potential units' or 'play units'. A potential unit is an empty space defined in part or surrounded by a tangible boundary. In a natural outdoor playspace this translates to the space under a tree, a grassy patch, a bushy den or a paved area. Play units are further classified as simple, complex or super units. Simple units have only one obvious use such as a swing or tricycle and, if used inappropriately, can become a safety hazard. Complex units incorporate two different play materials, which invite the child to manipulate or improvise, such as sand with cooking utensils. A super unit juxtaposes three or more play materials such as sand, water and cooking utensils. A natural outdoor playspace can be described as a smorgasbord of potential units and super units for children, a smorgasbord brimming with opportunities for manipulation. For example, a trickle stream with rocks, planks and boats, a digging patch with pipes, wheelbarrows and work hats or a dirt mound with boxes, planks and tyres are all super units. Super units 'accommodate the most children at one time and holds their interest longest' (Kritchevsky and Prescott, 1977, p 12). Potential units can become complex units and complex units can become super units with the addition of props and other loose materials.

3. What is the range of ages and abilities of the children who will be using the space? Will the outdoor playspace be shared? Both of these aspects will impact on the selection of materials and the organisation of the timetable for the day/session.

Anyone who has worked in an outdoor playspace where the age range and abilities of children is diverse can quickly list the associated issues and dilemmas:

- safety;
- providing challenge;
- wheel toys; and
- group games.

In a structured playspace with considerable fixed equipment, little variation in ground surfaces and minimal landscaping, these issues are often exacerbated. With regard to shared playspaces, Greenman and Stonehouse (1997, p 44) state that 'if the age range extends beyond 18 months, caregivers have to be more skilled to provide a program that is appropriate for all children in the group. It is a challenge to provide the range of materials, equipment, and experiences needed by children of diverse ages within one space'.

A natural playspace has the potential to defuse some of these challenging situations. Take the example of wheel toys, often a source of conflict and safety concerns (particularly bikes and tricycles for over 3-year-olds). In a natural outdoor playspace with an 'authentic aura' there are other options to consider. For example, small and large wheelbarrows suitable for toddlers up to 5-year-olds, hand trolleys for carting blocks and boxes and child-sized shopping-type trolleys, strollers or pushers for transporting dolls and loose materials. Clearly defined areas such as a gravel pit or digging patch for the wheelbarrows and a paved area for blocks and block trolleys will minimise random spreading of the equipment throughout the playspace. Clearly defined meandering paths with entrances and exits for pushers and trolleys will reduce the potential for collisions.

Other suggestions, noted by Berry (2001, p 37), include:

- keeping fixed structures to a minimum;
- providing a second sandpit for younger children;
- ensuring swing frames can fit a variety of swing attachments; and
- incorporating flexible areas such as low decking, bush cubbies, fallen tree logs, a clump of tree stumps, cosy corners and amphitheatres.

4. How much time in a single block?

Natural playspaces are not designed for a '10 minute run to let off steam' they are a work in progress designed to engage children and require their input. This can only happen if adequate periods of time are available. This applies equally to babies, toddlers and pre-school aged groups.

The early childhood literature commonly refers to the desirability of 'long periods' of time for outdoor play. Whilst it is essential to be flexible in any children's program, the impreciseness of what constitutes a 'long period' means that it can be misconstrued. In a setting where the timetable is rigidly defined, where children spend numerous periods throughout the day being grouped together for the same activity and loose materials are minimal (thus limiting the potential for engaging, sustained play to develop) half an hour might be considered a 'long period of time'. Crook and Farmer (2002, p 24) state 'a child needs approximately one hour of uninterrupted time to become familiar with play materials and explore a wide range of ideas'. Berry's reflection on ideal outdoor settings (2001, p 122) where children have the opportunity to 'explore, experiment and problem-solve, time to construct, develop dramatic play themes or socialise in a non-regimented environment' appears to support Crook and Farmer's suggestion. In some centres long periods of time outdoors might be most of a session or day. This extended outdoor time should be viewed positively by staff and parents if indoor and outdoor playspaces are viewed as equally valid learning environments. Ultimately, staff observations of children's level of engagement in play should provide a guide to the definition of 'long periods of time'.

5. Is indoor/outdoor a possibility?

Hopefully, the days of lining children up at the door to venture outdoors are gone. More child-centred approaches to program planning invite a greater understanding of the need for flexible routines, minimal transitions and large blocks (one hour minimum) of uninterrupted time for play. It seems both logical and desirable that children are able to have some choice in the matter of whether they play inside or outside. Adequate ratios and supervision can be maintained when an indoor/outdoor program is offered and such a program is well suited to the engaging natural outdoor playspace. A transition area like a verandah blurs the edges between indoor and outdoor and promotes seamless integration for indoor/outdoor programs.

6. What spontaneous opportunities can be anticipated?
A natural outdoor playspace has in-built qualities that support spontaneous play and some specific examples have been given earlier in the chapter. Nonetheless the environment needs to be prepared for both planned experiences and to support the interests and explorations that arise from free play.

For example, a group of children have observed that water seeps quickly into the sand and become frustrated in their to-ing and fro-ing from the water tank transferring containers of water that disappear quickly! Two scenarios might develop from this:

1. an adult might use this observation to plan a specific experience and prepare the sandpit by digging holes and lining them to create 'pools'; or
2. the children might work through the problem themselves or seek adult assistance for ideas.

In either scenario, access to a range of carefully selected and easily accessed open-ended resources by staff and children is essential. Pool liners could be improvised from vinyl off-cuts, plastic drop sheets, tubs or tyres; marine and freshwater animal models, rocks and weeds might be added for imaginative play; siphons, pumps and tubes for a science experience; glass stones or small tiles; small planks; people figures and so on.

7. What loose materials are available?
A natural outdoor playspace produces its own loose materials. These become perfect 'in situ' props for a multitude of uses such as dramatic and imaginative play or maths and science experiences. Leaf litter, gum nuts, sticks, leaves, bark peelings, fallen petals or blossoms, grass clippings, weeds and dirt can be considered when planning a program and have the added bonus that they do not require adults to source.

8. And, finally, is the total environment balanced?
All quality early childhood programs should offer a range and balance of play opportunities. In a natural outdoor playspace these include opportunities for fine and gross motor development, dramatic play, imaginative play, group games, art experiences, sensory play, science and maths experiences and so on. Solitary, parallel, associative, and co-operative play opportunities should be available at all times.

A sheltered verandah can become a place for impromptu connection with nature at Kidsfirst Mount Pleasant Kindergarten, Christchurch, NZ.

Improvising natural outdoor playspaces

Where the outdoor playspace is limited in terms of natural features, staff may feel disadvantaged in their endeavours to connect children with nature. The following photographs illustrate how it is possible to improvise natural playspaces. In addition, the natural loose parts to support play may not always be available and these could be collected with care from elsewhere. Suggested collections include gum nuts, leaves, small branches, stones, cones and pods (checking size so as not to be a potential choking hazard).

Improvisation with a wooden crate at Kidsfirst Beryl Mc Coombs Kindergarten, Christchurch, New Zealand, has created this productive garden. Also, consider old laundry baskets, tyres or other containers in smaller spaces, they have the added advantage of being moveable according to play needs and the weather.

Tyres (or portable planter boxes) can be used to divide a playspace, redirect traffic flow and for gardening experiences. Herbs, flowers and vegetables all grow well.

An old plastic container becomes a moveable colourful garden.

Dull and difficult spaces can be enlivened with some pots, tyres and logs for imaginative play.

Supporting planning with adequate storage

Adequate secure storage in outdoor playspaces is often overlooked and yet is a critical factor in the adults' capacity to effectively resource both planned and spontaneous play experiences. The need of children to also safely access a range of materials is an important consideration as is the occupational health and safety needs of staff.

It may seem obvious but, when staff (and children):

- know what equipment and materials are available;
- know where they are;
- can reach them easily and safely; and
- return them to the same place,

then the use of available resources will be maximised and the potential to accumulate vast amounts of rarely used materials is minimised. Staff will be reluctant to even enter outdoor storage areas that have combinations of inadequate lighting, shelving, signage, drainage, difficult doors and door openings, lack of ventilation, inappropriate locations and are unclean. Not only is there potential for stress reduction for staff when good storage systems are set in place, but there are benefits for children as well. Prescott (quoted in Greenman, 1998, p 125) 'found that organized storage led to more complex and longer lasting play'.

Developing ideas around storage 'systems' in conjunction with the traditional storage shed might help to alleviate some of the problems associated with poor outdoor storage. In a natural setting, careful consideration should be given to the selection of materials and design of any storage system. 'Soft natural timber that blends with the environment, or materials that are aesthetically pleasing, are desirable' (Walsh, 1991, p 94). Innovative storage structures can become part of the overall playspace design. For example, timber sandpit edges with top opening cupboards, narrow storage cupboards with shelving that opens externally to the playspace or bench seating that doubles as a storage box. Also, creative ideas such as branch stands for holding hats, coats or gum boots can be incorporated. It is worth noting that natural playspaces inherently contain so many play opportunities such that the storage of copious amounts of equipment is unnecessary.

This storage cupboard is part of the sandpit at Lady Gowrie Child Centre Melbourne.

The narrow shelves ensure easy access and labelling promotes the return of all materials. A wooden storage space complements the natural outdoor space.

Planning for Children in Natural Playspaces   < 149 >

This wooden storage shed has a small lockable door for putting planks away.

< 150 >   The Outdoor Playspace Naturally

References

Arthur L, Beecher B, Death E, Dockett S and Farmer S, 2005, *Programming and Planning in Early Childhood Settings*, 3rd ed, Nelson, Sydney, Australia.

Baldwin Dancy R, 2000, *You Are Your Child's First Teacher*, Celestial Arts, California, USA.

Berry P, 2001, *Playgrounds that Work. Creating Outdoor Play Environments for Children Birth to Eight Years*, Pademelon Press, Sydney, Australia.

Crook S and Farmer B, 2002, *Just Imagine*, 2nd ed, Tertiary Press, Croydon, Victoria.

Fleer M, Ed, 1995, DAP *Centrism Challenging Developmentally Appropriate Practice*, Australian Early Childhood Association, Canberra, Australia.

Fleer M and Richardson C, 2004, *Observing and Planning in Early Childhood Settings: Using a Sociocultural Approach*, Early Childhood Australia Inc. Canberra, Australia.

Gardner H, 1983, *Frames of Mind: The Theory of Multiple Intelligences*, Basic Books, New York.

Gardner H, 1999, *Intelligence Re-Framed*, Basic Books, New York.

Greenman J, 1998, *Caring Spaces, Learning Places: Children's Environments That Work*, Exchange Press, Redmond, WA, USA.

Greenman J and Stonehouse A, 1997, *Prime Times A Handbook for Excellence in Infant and Toddler Programs*, Addison Wesley Longman, Sydney, Australia.

Kritchevsky S and Prescott E, 1977, *Planning Environments for Young Children Physical Space*, NAEYC, Washington, USA.

Lunt C and Williamson D, 1999, *Children's Experiences Folio*, RMIT Publishing, Melbourne, Australia.

Rogoff B, 1990, *Apprenticeship in Thinking: Cognitive Development in Social Context*, Oxford University Press, New York.

Walsh P, 1991, *Early Childhood Playgrounds: Planning an Outside Learning Environment*, Pademelon Press, Sydney, Australia.

Bibliography

Jaffke F, 1991, *Work and Play in Early Childhood*, Floris Books, Edinburgh, Scotland.

Petrash C, 1993, *Earthwise: Environmental Crafts and Activities with Young Children*, Floris Books, Edinburgh, Scotland.

Young T and Elliott S, 2003, *Just Investigate: Science and Technology Experiences for Young Children*, Tertiary Press, Croydon, Victoria.

Young T and Elliott S, 2004, *Just Discover: Connecting Young Children with the Natural World*, Tertiary Press, Croydon, Victoria.

Useful resources

- The Bureau of Meteorology produces an Australian Weather Calendar each year. Each month depicts a different weather condition and has a beautiful large photograph accompanied by useful information. For more information go to www.bom.gov.au/calendar/
- The Australian Geographic Shop sells a range of publications and resources related to weather and exploring nature, suitable for use with young children. For your nearest supplier look in the business section of the telephone directory.
- There are suppliers of Steiner play materials and publications in each state. Typical of the publications are Petrash (1993) and Jaffke (1991), which contain many ideas for play experiences related to each season for children 3 years plus.

Early childhood centre
case studies from
Australia

Sue Elliott

8

Introduction

The eleven Australian case studies documented in this chapter illustrate the diversity of early childhood programs, cultures and geographic locations from a remote Indigenous childcare and preschool in Northern Territory to an inner urban kindergarten within a school in Melbourne. When identifying centres to include here, the main criterion was the natural outdoor playspace. However, the stories revealed in the case studies describe a richness of experience beyond mere trees, rocks and logs. Themes emerge not only about connections with nature, but about collective action, collaborative processes and a sense of ownership and identity. Each case study provides practical insight and demonstrates a depth of commitment to natural outdoor playspaces. Be inspired!

Clovelly Child Care Centre

Maria Pender—Director

The community-managed centre provides long day care for 55 children from babies to 5-year-olds. The children are cared for in three age groupings, babies, 2- to 3-year-olds and 3- to 5-year-olds and each group has access to an outdoor playspace. The centre is located in an outer urban area of Sydney close to the beach and on a sloping site.

Impetus for a natural playspace

The impetus for changes in the playspaces towards more natural playspaces stems from the educational belief of the Director that children in care should have access to the most natural of settings possible to facilitate play.

The process of change

All three playspaces have now been redeveloped to create natural settings for play. The most recent work has been completed in the 3- to 5-year-olds' playspace, but was initially conceived six years ago. It took five years to raise approximately $50 000 to undertake the work and the parent committee was very supportive of the project. The playspace designer, Ric McConaghy, was employed to design a space that reflected the centre philosophy and the space available. The actual development work took about four weeks to complete and children became very involved observing and documenting the construction process.

Playspace features include

- all three playspaces have sandpits;
- sandstone and timber predominates in edging, retaining walls and seating;
- one playspace has an interactive sandstone water feature that children can operate;
- a wooden bridge;
- a boat;
- many established trees and recent plantings;
- a memorial fairy garden established by a parent; and
- textural shapes cast in concrete on the ground.

Benefits and outcomes

The children's creative and imaginative play has been enhanced by the new playspace features. For example, the bridge, boat and sandstone rocks have promoted fishing and pirate play.

Goals for the future

Most of the work envisaged has been completed; however, three items need further work—a small garden in an exit area, a totem pole and a vegetable garden.

Concerns

Rubber soft-fall occurs in a few parts of the playspace and some has been removed during the redevelopment. Staff have found it problematic over time due to the heat, smell, potential to cause grazing and difficulty of cleaning.

Final words of advice for other centres considering a natural playspace

The Director believes that professional design has been important to ensure a good outcome overall and create an inviting natural playspace. We have walked and played on dirt, grass and rocks for thousands of years and this is what children need!

Textural shapes in the concrete create sensory interest.

Dry creek bed with sandstone boulders and wooden bridge.

Sandstone water feature for children to access water.

< 156 >   The Outdoor Playspace Naturally

Campus Kindergarten

Robert Pratt—Kindergarten Teacher

Campus Kindergarten (CK) provides long day care and sessional preschool at the University of Queensland, St Lucia campus in urban Brisbane. A total of 63 children from diverse cultures and ranging in age from $2\frac{1}{2}$ to 6 years attend the centre each day.

Impetus for a natural playspace

CK has long been a green space due to its location in an urban green belt that encompasses the University of Queensland. However, it was during a staff professional development day in early 1997 that a common interest in the environment was identified. The staff team at the time were also looking for an opportunity to develop a 'team building project' that could create a greater sense of community and collaboration at CK. Hence, the 'Sustainable Planet Project' was born. From that moment the CK community have had a strong focus on enhancing their natural outdoor playspace and developing Environmental Education programs.

The process of change

Development of the natural outdoor playspace has been very much a community project; encouraging active participation by all community members—children, teachers, parents and the broader community. Throughout the project there have been at least a handful of people (mostly teachers) who have taken more active leadership roles; maintaining momentum and organising projects etc.

There have been no specific budget items with regards to expenditure; the annual centre budget has made some provision for ongoing minor costs. No significant purchases have been required to date as the centre has made use of free community resources—for example, Brisbane City Council free plants scheme—and most of the work in creating the playspace has been carried out by the children, teachers and parents at no cost.

Almost all of the ongoing care and maintenance of the playspace is carried out by community members and embedded into the everyday program and practices at CK.

Playspace features include

- large outdoor playspace comprising grassed and soft fall areas, sand and mud pits, and rocks;
- many established native trees, some suitable for climbing and others inhabited by wildlife (birds, possums, and so on);
- many garden beds of native shrubs and grasses creating screens and private playspaces;
- natural materials used for garden edging including rocks, bamboo and logs;
- native bee, bird and possum boxes and a frog pond to attract wildlife;
- permanent climbing equipment and swings are made of wood rather than plastic;
- a vegetable garden and other edible and scented plants, with plans for fruit trees;
- a chicken coop;
- composting equipment and worm farms; and
- indoor and outdoor spaces that flow together seamlessly.

Benefits and outcomes

The development of a natural playspace with greater biodiversity has provided the CK community with a pleasant place to live and learn. In fact it has become a learning environment, a place where we all have opportunities to connect with nature enabling us to develop our awareness, knowledge and love of the environment. Many of the adults and children have developed a greater sense of responsibility for the environment and have felt motivated and empowered to take actions resulting in environmental improvement.

Goals for the future

The development of the Environmental Education program and the outdoor playspace is an evolving process. Some specific goals include:

- improving the overall aesthetics by planting more native plants, particularly established trees, and the removal of the last remaining 'weed' species;
- accessing University of Queensland recycled water for irrigation and upgrading the current irrigation system to be more water efficient;
- installing water tanks and investigating the possibilities of a system to collect storm water run off for irrigation;
- extending the vegetable garden and chook area to create space for fruit trees and more chooks; and
- maintaining and or replacing the outdoor climbing equipment

Concerns

A constant challenge, particularly with recent drought conditions, has been ensuring adequate irrigation as we tried to establish new plants. Plans are now in place, as described above, to alleviate this situation.

Also, we are mindful of ensuring that our playspace complies with relevant regulations.

Final words of advice for other centres considering a natural playspace

- access support and knowledge from all community members, including the broader community;
- encourage active participation by all community members;
- take small steps, set goals but aim to achieve them one or two at a time;
- a supportive co-ordinator or leader helps with organisation and maintaining momentum; and
- view challenges as learning opportunities.

Mature trees create inviting shady playspaces.

Children are involved daily in caring for the playspace.

Clunes Community Preschool

Melinda Gambley—Director

The Clunes Community Preschool is located in a small town on the northern NSW coast. The centre has 20 children aged 3 to 5 years attending daily. The location is semi rural and many families are escapees from capital cities seeking alternative lifestyles. The preschool is situated on a steeply sloping quarter acre block.

Impetus for a natural playspace

The preschool community values the natural environment and wanted to create opportunities for the children to interact with natural materials and small animals in the environment. Also, to create a space that was aesthetically pleasing—calming and relaxing for children, parents and staff, with the potential for children to be creative and follow their own interests

The process of change

The parent management committee, staff and the director were all involved in creating the playspace. The preschool community was clear that they didn't want a prefabricated, static playspace, but rather something open-ended that was sympathetic to the surroundings. Also, it was clear that there were many features in the playspace to be retained including established trees, terracing and two sandpits. Initially, staff and the director read widely, viewed other playspaces (both in centres and public playspaces) and sought the paid advice of a Kidsafe consultant. A landscape designer was employed to pull together the ideas on paper. When the actual work began, the landscape designer supervised the completion of the structural and landscaping parts of the project, organised workers and materials and scheduled the major parts of the job. Also, a builder was employed to construct the structural parts. It took a year to complete (work was mostly undertaken in the school holiday breaks) and cost approximately $30 000.

Playspace features include

- retaining walls and planted banks that create three flat areas and a creek bed on the steep slope;
- three flat areas containing fixed play equipment such as swings, a hardwood cubbyhouse/stage area, a concrete bike track and a softfall area for moveable climbing equipment;
- a sloping creek bed that can be used wet or dry;
- several established trees providing good shade coverage as well as loose materials (leaves, bark, flowers, seeds etc) for creative play;
- gardens with textured or scented plants and plants that provide flowers or leaves for dramatic and imaginative play;
- a vegetable and herb garden; and
- an abundance of loose surface materials including medium and small rocks, fine pebbles, sand and dirt.

Benefits and outcomes

The goal of an aesthetically pleasing and soothing space for all who come to the preschool has been achieved. This is evident in the children's play and the positive response of parents and staff to the playspace.

The variety of natural loose materials enhances children's imaginative play in many ways. For example, a smooth rock from the creek bed becomes a fish in a pretend fishing expedition or a cake at a birthday picnic and leaves or flowers can be collected to become gifts for hospital play, wedding bouquets or ingredients for wombat stew.

There are now many more animals in the playspace to observe including birds, small lizards, frogs, beetles and caterpillars. Underneath the rocks, slaters and earthworms are just waiting to be discovered! This has greatly enhanced opportunities to observe the natural world and led to discussions, investigations and research.

Goals for the future

Currently there are two goals:

■ add more textured/scented/edible plants; and
■ add more plants and water sources for the small animals, lizards and birds that are now in abundance.

Concerns

One concern is to develop a system to successfully and safely recycle the water from the creek bed. Water conservation is a priority and as yet we have been unsuccessful in this respect.

Final words of advice for other centres considering a natural playspace

■ spend lots of time researching and planning;
■ it may be worth spending money to consult with some specialists at the early stages;
■ find tradespeople who understand what you are trying to achieve;
■ aim to have spaces that are flexible and suited to more than one purpose; and
■ include loose materials in your playspace, they are fundamental to play.

Rocks to clamber over and look under for garden bugs.

Coburg Children's Centre

Michelle Hocking—Program Planning Co-ordinator

The Coburg Children's Centre is a community-based long day care centre registered for 62 children with three children's rooms. Coburg is a north-western suburb of metropolitan Melbourne and a culturally and linguistically diverse group of families are enrolled at the centre.

Impetus for a natural playspace

The move towards a natural playspace was, in some ways, an extension of features already in existence. Mature eucalypts provided good shade, plantings of hardy shrubs created some definition of playspaces and the overall size of the space was relatively large with minimal fixed equipment. The impetus for a natural playspace arose from a timely combination of events.

The process of change

The playspace has been a work in progress for some 12 years. Staff wanted to address a range of issues: children running (or riding trikes) in and through areas where other children were settled in play; storage and cleaning of equipment issues; program planning for the outdoors; respectful use of equipment by the children; and poor drainage resulting in pools of water after rain. In 1995 a small group of staff formed the 'Outdoor Action Group' to address these issues and discuss ideas for re-development. It was felt that the design of the space contributed to some of the problems. For example, directly adjacent to the exits from the playrooms was a large area of artificial grass surrounded by a concrete path. The space sent a clear message to the children 'start running when you come out the door and don't stop!'.

Aesthetically the space was one of real contrasts, mature plantings, an enormous concrete 'bunker' used for storage, concrete paths and large areas of grass worn away to dirt. One of the staff in the group was involved in the organisation Environmental Education in Early Childhood Vic. Inc. (EEEC). As a result of visits to other centres with the EEEC group (Attwood Children's Centre, St Kilda and Balaclava Kindergarten, Bond St Kindergarten and One World for Children Centre), a number of suggestions were brought back to the Outdoor Action Group for consideration. An early childhood consultant, Sue Crook, was employed to provide professional development for the staff in program planning, toy making and imaginative play. This had an immediate, positive impact on the development of the space and program planning throughout the centre.

Staff developed a wish list that was presented to the coordinator and board of management who were very supportive. An amount of $30 000 was budgeted for over a three-year period ($10 000 each year). A landscape architect was employed to draw up the plans and the work commenced in 1996. The work comprised major excavation to address drainage issues and the installation of a trickle stream, secret area, perfumed garden, digging patch, a new swing frame, second sandpit and children's garden beds. Playspaces were divided by mass planting; pathways and a variety of ground surfaces were incorporated. In 1999 the concrete bunker was demolished and the space converted to a soft fall area and storage shed. Numerous small projects have been undertaken since that time.

The outdoor playspace consists of two separate play areas divided by an internal fence.

Features of the smaller space used by the younger children include

- ground surfaces such as slate paving, timber decking, concrete, artificial grass, dirt and small patches of tufted grass;
- two sandpits, one sunken and one at ground level separated by two medium height shrubs with enough space between to create a 'living' tunnel. The sunken sandpit is extended on one side by a section of timber decking; and
- recent projects have seen the improvement of the outdoor storage system, now a wide shallow set of cupboards opening externally to the playspace (multiple narrow shelves enable all the equipment to be seen); and the replacement of a portion of artificial grass with a raised timber deck.

Features of the larger space include

- mass planting ranging from very mature trees, to medium height shrubs through to grasses, climbers, ground covers and flowers in boxes. Plantings are used to define and divide playspaces as well as contribute significantly to the overall 'natural' feel of the space;
- a trickle stream lined with river stones that uses reticulated water
- a digging patch;
- a wooden bridge;
- two sandpits (one at ground level free form in shape bordered by plantings, the other more geometric in shape bordered by a raised timber deck);
- an amphitheatre;
- an ornamental grape vine-covered pergola and shelter;
- simple timber seating;
- various gardens such as a children's garden, secret garden (not so secret since a mature wattle was uprooted during a recent storm!), perfumed garden, and plant hospital;
- a water tank;
- a worm farm;
- three timber storage sheds;
- a variety of ground surfaces such as bare soil, compacted granitic sand, tan bark, eucalyptus mulch, concrete, timber decking, log rounds, paving (slate and brick), artificial grass, log rounds and rock;
- low trellis and sections of picket fencing divide areas and support the growth of climbing plants and shrubs; and
- mosaic leaf printed tiles created by a parent with the older children are scattered over seating, pathways and borders throughout the space.

Benefits and outcomes

Children have the opportunity to be engaged in real work in the fresh air. This not only has physical health benefits and contributes to the development of specific skills, but also makes a genuine contribution to the overall maintenance of the space and promotes a sense of ownership. This applies equally to staff as well as the children. When the children move outdoors they have very clear visual messages about their play options and pathways. Children have the opportunity to learn about life cycles and the interdependence of plants, animals and humans. It is hoped that their experiences in this playspace will be the catalyst for life-long environmental sensitivity and awareness.

Goals for the future

Someone once said that good playgrounds never actually finish and this is the philosophy at the Coburg Children's Centre. Plans for future developments in

A water tank is accessible for children and the worm farm is located nearby.

A combined planter box and toddler seat defines the corner of the timber decking.

the smaller playspace include a small dry creek bed, planting of mature trees to improve shade and a bamboo feature wall. In the larger space, the concrete paths will need maintenance and the small remaining area of artificial grass is looking well worn. A second ornamental grape vine is being trained over verandah wire to create shade and this will take another year to provide adequate cover. With the loss of the wattle the secret garden needs to be re-considered, another wattle or perhaps another water feature?

Mature trees, pot plants and various garden beds create a natural feel to the playspace.

Concerns

Some of the trees have lost limbs in storms and several others have been assessed by a horticulturalist as having a limited life span. This is a reminder that the space needs to be prepared now for the next generation of children who will use it. New trees have been planted in the vicinity of the mature ones as future replacements.

Final words of advice for other centres considering a natural playspace

- make a wish list of desired features;
- visit as many other centres as possible with these features to compare and contrast designs; and
- ask questions, take photographs, talk to the staff who work in the space, and observe children playing in the space if possible.

Doncaster Kindergarten

Sally Dent—Director

Doncaster Kindergarten is a council-owned and parent-managed kindergarten located in middle urban Melbourne. It offers sessional preschool programs for 40 children aged 3 to 4 years and 40 children aged 4 to 5 years. Also, the kindergarten community includes a diverse range of cultures.

Impetus for a natural playspace

The previous director, Ann Smith, began the rainforest garden project to develop a serene and natural environment within the outdoor playspace. The aim was to promote imaginative play and positive environmental attitudes and provide a place for seclusion. Ann had also noted that many children's books focused on tropical rainforest and she believed it was important to create Victorian temperate rainforest as a more relevant experience for the children.

The process of change

Ann researched the types of plants suited to a temperate rainforest garden, consulted with the local council and prepared a sketch plan. The most appropriate site for the garden was determined by several mature shady native trees, these would help to create the required microclimate. The kindergarten was successful in obtaining an Exon-Mobil grant to purchase the required plants and the parent committee was very supportive. A family working bee was organised to create the garden and Ann also worked with the children to establish the garden. They planted three tree ferns, other smaller ferns and sacred bamboo as a screening plant. Later, a watering system was installed to ensure the plants survived the dry summers.

Playspace features include

- rainforest garden of tree ferns, shade plants and over arching trees;
- a meandering crushed gravel pathway down the middle of the garden;
- logs for the children to sit on or incorporate in play; and
- a cubby at the end of the pathway.

Benefits and outcomes

- the rainforest garden is a visually cool area within the playspace and is particularly beneficial on hot days;
- the rainforest garden is a place for quiet imaginative play, seclusion, reflection and exploration by the children;
- parents often comment on the attractiveness of the playspace; and
- both children and staff find the rainforest garden an inviting area.

Goals for the future

The rainforest garden will continue to be a work in progress as children, staff and parents maintain the garden and add or replace plants.

Concerns

Initially, watering was a concern; but as the plants become established and a microclimate develops, the need for watering will lessen. Also, there has been a higher incidence of mosquitoes around the garden and, to alleviate this, the intention is to plant some mosquito repelling plants.

Final words of advice for other centres considering a natural playspace

- an outdoor playspace is an on-going project and never finished;
- balancing your playspace vision with views of others and what is financially possible requires compromise;
- parents are a great resource of voluntary workers, make use of them;
- depending on location, schedule the planting for winter or spring, our planting was a little later so watering quickly became a concern over the summer holidays; and
- search for grants to support the project, management committees may have other funding priorities and are more likely to offer support for the project if grant money is available.

East Bairnsdale Early Learning Centre

Jo Nunn—Director

East Bairnsdale Early Learning Centre offers a flexible hours model kindergarten program and occasional care for approximately 50 children aged 3 to 5 years. The double unit centre is located on the fringes of Bairnsdale, a rural city in East Gippsland, Victoria. Jo Nunn has been the director of the centre for 28 years.

Impetus for a natural playspace

The design of the playspace is fundamentally the same as when the centre was established 28 years ago. The playspace is very large and has many mature native trees; both original trees and many that have been planted over the years. The rural landscape itself was in many ways the impetus for the natural playspace.

The process of change

On-going planting has created a very green and naturally aesthetic playspace. In addition, the children's interests with support from staff and families have led to the creation of the rainforest area, butterfly enclosure and frog pond. Although shady trees abound, a pergola with creepers was erected to provide shade specifically over the sandpit. Also, the tan bark area was extended to accommodate the flexible climbing equipment in accordance with regulatory requirements. Parents, children, staff and tradespeople have been involved at various times in creating the changes in the playspace.

Playspace features include

- an extensive physical area that has a range of open and quiet spaces inviting small and large group experiences;
- a seasonal butterfly enclosure;
- a frog pond and fernery adjacent to an Indigenous mural;
- a large sand area that promotes exploration and extension of play ideas;
- a digging patch;
- large open grassed areas;
- a rainforest area;
- flexible and open-ended spaces that can be developed according to specific creative learning experiences and play ideas;
- opportunities for children to link play between areas such as the rainforest and digging patch;
- a green cubby made from a rose arbour planted with a soft leaf creeper;
- a worm farm, compost and flexible areas for growing vegetables (they use old pots and tyres for growing and move them according to the seasons);
- a shady courtyard with access to outdoor power for using equipment such as high powered magnifiers and portable light boxes for investigative work;
- an equipment shed designed for children to access materials as needed for indoor or outdoor play; and
- a variety of playspaces over a large area so that intrusion into other children's play is unlikely.

Benefits and outcomes

- the design of the centre invites opportunities to link the indoor experiences to the outdoor environment, thus promoting a flexible and integrated program;

- significant periods of time outside in the playspace are part of each day. Jo believes when the children have long periods of engagement in outdoor experiences the concentration is more intent, particularly for the boys in the group;
- spending time outside at the beginning of each day makes for more relaxed and engaged children indoors later in the day;
- also, beginning outdoors allows for the unravelling of 'morning family life styles' in an atmosphere where the naturalness of the outdoors provides space and time for connection and feeling a sense of place;
- children respond positively and imaginatively to the flexibility of the play-space and opportunities to recreate play areas to meet their specific play needs—designing, creating and using spaces for themselves;
- space and flexibility means that traditional indoor experiences are often taken outdoors and used in different ways by different children; and
- children emotionally connect with the environment—the living spaces the wildlife and smaller creatures—and have opportunities to create habitats.

Goals for the future

- the re-creation within the playspace of some local landscapes and habitats of the East Gippland region such as wetlands and coastal areas;
- a bush tucker garden reflecting local Indigenous culture; and
- a specific outdoor laboratory to connect scientific 'facts' and environmental education with the 'passions and interests' that children bring to the centre.

Concerns

- the centre was built at the bottom of a hill and there have been on-going drainage problems which are slowly being rectified;
- the verandah could connect the indoor and outdoor areas more effectively to facilitate indoor/outdoor play; and
- securing funding for new projects is a continuing challenge.

The leafy cubby has been created by growing a flowering passion-fruit vine over a rose arbour. It can be pruned as needed and adds to the loose parts available for play.

The large sandpit has a timber border and a variety of re-usable items are available for play.

Children, staff and parents worked together to create the fernery and frog pond. The indigenous mural is relevant to the local area.

Final words of advice for other centres considering a natural playspace

Remember all children need large spaces for physical experiences such as running, rolling and ball play, and open spaces where they can construct with their own materials and change the play focus as desired. They still need fixed swings, but also flexible movable climbing equipment that can be rearranged, varied and adapted as required.

Natural playspaces invite children to express their creativity and learning and this is a fundamental need for everyone, not just children. This builds our relationship with the natural environment that informs our sense of what it is to be human.

Create opportunities for children to feel the grass between their toes!

Butterflies are attracted to the specific plants in the centre butterfly enclosure. Once butterfly eggs have been observed on the plants, the shade cloth sides are secured to hooks on the four top timber edges. Children, staff and parents can visit the butterfly enclosure to observe the life cycle stages, then the butterflies are released when the sides are removed again. The butterfly enclosure can be used for other play experiences the remainder of the year.

Kinma Preschool

Jacqui Besso—Early Childhood Teacher

Kinma is an independent parent-managed preschool and provides a preschool program four days per week for children aged between 3 and 5 years. The centre is licensed for up to 39 children per day and also has a parent managed playgroup one day each week. The preschool is located within an independent primary school and located close to farmland and a national park on the outer fringes of Sydney in Terrey Hills.

Impetus for a natural playspace

When Kinma was originally purchased, the staff and parent body at that time had a strong connection to and respect for the natural environment. Stemming from these values, the preschool and school outdoor environments were designed to facilitate children's love of nature by incorporating the natural bushland into the playspaces and these are still enjoyed today.

The process of change

Kinma has a dynamic, ever changing and evolving community and thus both indoors and outdoors are constantly developing to meet the needs and interests of new children, staff and parents. The outdoor environment changes year by year as parent groups, children and staff work together on working bees and school maintenance days to nurture and care for the outdoor environment. Parents and staff donate their time, skills, and resources to the natural environment, thus all have a greater ownership and commitment to Kinma and its surroundings.

Playspace features include

- Kinma is surrounded by native bushland and staff maximise the potential of the natural environment as a learning tool by including bushwalks and expeditions into the surrounding community as regular events in the program;
- a natural creek running alongside the outer perimeter of the preschool is a source of tadpoles, frogs and insects and invites many hours of play immersed in the natural environment;
- the extensive grounds include several sandpits, rope swings, climbing trees, a native garden, a worm farm, composting area and no-dig vegetable beds;
- at various times of the year the preschool is home to a variety of animals such as chickens, guinea pigs, rabbits, possums, lizards, frogs, birds and snakes;
- the obstacle course changes regularly and is made of mostly reused items donated by families. Old tyres are used as stepping stones, ropes for balancing along, ladders for climbing and wooden planks for balance beams;
- one parent donated an old canoe which is now a vegetable garden and another old dinghy is used in the sandpit as a stimulus for dramatic play; and
- several of the vegetable garden beds are even made of old tractor tyres. We find as many ways to reuse things in our playspace as possible.

Benefits and outcomes

The benefits of such a unique, natural playspace are many and varied. Surrounded by nature, the children are able to build up their knowledge, familiarity and appreciation of the natural world around them. Respect and care for their environment is facilitated by the incorporation of authentic experiences such as composting, worm farming, animal care, recycling, gardening and

bushwalking in the preschool program. Important life-skills and attitudes are influenced and nurtured in the children who attend the preschool. Also, adults are able to role model positive attitudes and love of the natural environment through their care of and commitment to the Kinma grounds. Children and adults work alongside one another, thus communicating joint respect and ownership of the Kinma environment. In today's society, with larger homes/town houses and smaller gardens and less playspace, it is very important to offer children a natural play environment.

Goals for the future

Kinma is and always will be a work in progress. This is part of the beauty of a parent-run school—the talent and resource pool of parents and staff is forever growing and changing, new skills are gained, adults teach one another and move forward to address issues facing the preschool. A new preschool facility is currently being built on Kinma land and parents have been heavily involved in sourcing resources for the building, donating equipment and time and developing the design. The new facility will reflect the ecologically-based philosophy of Kinma and demonstrate the Kinma community's respect for the natural environment and desire to minimise impact on the surrounding bushland.

Concerns

Along with the beauty of the natural setting enjoyed at Kinma comes a host of issues that could be considered the down sides of the unique setting:

- surrounded by native bushland, bushfire becomes a real hazard during the hotter and drier seasons. To counter this, a fire drill is practised routinely to equip children and staff with the knowledge to respond appropriately and minimise any physical threat to individuals;
- bush ticks live in the scrub and bushland and children and staff often find themselves prey to these arachnids. Both natural and chemically based preventative sprays are available to deter these pests as well as information on how to deal with and treat a tick bite;

- snakes and spiders also make their home in the surroundings. The staff choose to view them as learning tools as they teach children and adults to respect and live alongside nature peacefully. The staff regularly undertake first aid courses to ensure they up to date on the treatment of a snake or spider bite should one occur;
- a frustration rather than a concern is the possum that lives under the preschool. The possum loves Kinma as the preschool provides excellent shelter, a food source as well as a toilet for the possum and its family. Possum droppings and urine have to be cleaned up each morning, as the outdoor verandah is open for attack each night. However, the children love to observe and learn about the possum's habits as a nocturnal animal and find a lot of interest and joy in seeing it sleeping under the preschool; and
- the most important concern is the impact people have on the environment. Areas of heavy traffic and play result in dusty, barren patches of earth that can turn into a dust bowl if not managed effectively.

Final words of advice for other centres considering a natural playspace

The native bushland backdrop is a unique feature of Kinma preschool; this photo was taken prior to redevelopment of the site.

Talk to the children and find out their ideas and interests and remember you don't need big $$, just big imagination!

Princes Hill Preschool

Margaret Finch—Kindergarten Teacher

Princes Hill Preschool offers sessional preschool and/or extended hours programs for 83 4-year-old and 3-year-old children. This inner Melbourne preschool is managed by the City of Yarra and provides a service for a culturally diverse community. The preschool is co-located with a Maternal and Child Health centre in the grounds of Princes Hill Primary School.

Impetus for a natural playspace

The impetus has come from the location in a typical schoolyard in an inner urban area and trying to create a 'green oasis' for young children's play.

The process of change

A number of steps or tasks have facilitated the change process:
- the council installed a drinking fountain recycled from a local park;
- garden beds were extended to create 'garden rooms' for play areas;
- families donated plants that staff and children sorted into various garden beds – the rock garden, a perennial bed, herbs in tyres etc;
- various trees were planted for shade and interest – olive, Manchurian pear, wattle;
- the council placed tractor tyres over some of the pine poles and planted ornamental grapes which will grow to eventually replace the shade cloth (which is often damaged by vandalism);
- twelve large pots, soil and a large number of parsley, fennel, cabbage and pansy seedlings were donated. Staff and children planted the pots and also put some of the seedlings around the vines in the tractor tyres. Everyone enjoyed eating the parsley!; and
- a load of logs was donated and these have been used variously as edging to protect new planting and as seats.

Current features include:

- an open lawn area maintained by the council;
- various garden beds;
- a range of pot plants;
- a worm farm donated by the parents and a compost bin;
- two sandpits;
- a softfall tan bark area;
- a digging patch; and
- an outdoors eating area.

Benefits and outcomes

- the children are more aware of the seasons through observations of the plants and changes in the weather. They observe cloud patterns and feel when it is likely to rain;
- the staff are more relaxed working outdoors in a garden-like setting;
- children are able to play physical games such as soccer or engage in construction work in the open space and other children's play is not interrupted;
- children who have limited outdoor space at home can play in a large safe playspace and experience contact with nature;

- staff and children work together for the purpose of maintaining the garden, sharing both skills and values; and
- the smaller 'garden rooms' are utilised for various types of play and promote children's focus on the play for long periods of time.

Goals for the future

There are always goals for the future—staff and children are constantly working in the garden—weeding, sweeping, pruning, picking up litter and fallen twigs, as well as planting. More planting is planned to create further 'garden rooms', to provide wind protection and also privacy from the school.
Some further seating is needed too.

Concerns

- some of the concerns relate to the exposed location within the school grounds, everything must be packed away daily and vandalism is an on-going issue;
- wind whistles through the garden, as there is not enough shelter from the north, west and east; and
- outdoor play on rainy days is limited because there is no covered outdoor space.

Final words of advice for other centres considering a natural playspace

Ask for help from interested parents! Parents have helped with planting and maintaining garden beds, pruning, donating plants and purchasing a worm farm.

Also, it is stimulating to visit as many centres as possible both through Environmental Education in Early Childhood Vic Inc and other networking opportunities. It is interesting to see playspace ideas in other locations that can inspire further playspace development; for example, Bairnsdale Early Learning Centre and the Ian Potter Foundation Children's Garden at the Royal Botanic Gardens Melbourne.

The planted borders of hardy lavender and pelargonium help to create the 'green oasis'.

A variety of ground surfaces is important ... stone, brick, mosaic and grass are illustrated. Also, productive plants such as the herbs in tyres and the olive tree are part of the learning experience.

A chime bar for musical experiences.

The recycled water fountain from a nearby council park, now part of the preschool.

St Kilda and Balaclava Kindergarten

Mary McLoughlan—Co-ordinator

St Kilda and Balaclava Kindergarten was originally established in 1911 and has been located in the current building since its construction in 1925 (Smith, 2001). Today the kindergarten offers both long day care and sessional programs for children aged 3 to 5 years. The centre is registered for 55 places and is located in an inner Melbourne suburb.

Impetus for a natural playspace

The kindergarten has an on-going commitment to promoting and providing environmental education for children. The natural outdoor playspace is a demonstration of that commitment.

The process of change

Staff, families and friends of the kindergarten have contributed ideas, skills and manual labour since the kindergarten was established and the playspace has been constantly evolving since 1925.

Playspace features include

- a large playspace area;
- moveable wooden structures;
- various recycled materials, for example, tyres;
- an old row boat that is used as a garden bed;
- vegetable gardens;
- digging patches;
- fully established shady trees including a heritage listed peppercorn tree;
- various plantings of shrubs, grasses, flowers;
- large compost bins;
- many pot plants that can be moved to define smaller playspaces;
- tanbark softfall; and
- four water wall type rainwater tanks which children can collect water from.

Benefits and outcomes for children include

- understanding of the need to care for the environment;
- holistic learning about nature and the relationships between elements;
- gaining self-confidence and skills in body control in a physically challenging playspace;
- developing strategies for active exploration of the natural playspace; and
- links with the family and wider world are affirmed and extended.

Mature trees and flexible equipment create an inner urban oasis.

Goals for the future

The outdoor playspace is an area that will keep evolving with new staff and fresh ideas. The building and the garden have inspired early childhood educators to create natural playspaces for young children to explore, create and discover 'a slice of rural in an inner city environment'.

Final words of advice for other centres considering a natural playspace

- select equipment that is moveable to promote flexibility and to create relevant settings with inspirational and imaginative workspaces for staff and children;
- when selecting materials and equipment, choose natural and/or recycled materials over plastics; and
- actively seek staff with a commitment to environmental education and the use of open-ended natural playspaces.

Smith S, 2001, *Looking After the Little Ones the first 90 years of the St Kilda and Balaclava Kindergarten 1911–2001*, St Kilda and Balaclava Kindergarten, Balaclava.

Water tanks installed behind the sandpit and under the shade of the heritage listed peppercorn tree.

The much loved row boat has renewed life as a vegetable garden.

Terrigal Children's Centre

Bev Boys—Director

The centre is located in the Gosford City Council area in the central coast region north of Sydney, NSW, and provides long day care for 40 children from babies to 5-year-olds. The 15 children under 3 years and the 25 children over 3 years have separate outdoor playspaces, but a gate encourages visiting between friends and siblings. The playspace is large and shady and sited on a gentle slope with garden beds providing pockets for play.

Impetus for a natural playspace

A significant impetus for the natural playspace has been the children's ongoing interest in the centre's natural environment; for example, finding bugs, lizards, turtles and birds that visit regularly. Staff complement the children's interest by planning experiences; for example, planting, worm farming, composting, to encourage children's respect for and interaction with the natural environment. The changes in the playspace were supported by staff, children, families and the wider community and everyone worked together to achieve a positive outcome.

The process of change

Early in 2004 a staff meeting was held to discuss the playspace and the following points emerged:

- a need to foster an understanding and appreciation of our natural environment;
- the redesign of 'dead' play areas;
- a need for spaces to promote social interaction; and
- the conservation of resources.

Also in 2004, the centre became aware of the Gosford City Council's preschool sustainability program 'Little Green Steps'. Staff participated in professional development about sustainability and the centre received assistance to apply for rainwater tank funding.

The children were involved in plans to redesign the 'dead' areas of the playspace. Children and staff discussed and drew ideas about the changes they wanted to see in their playspace. The children suggested stepping stones, paintings on the fence, flowers, a dinosaur garden and water play activities. After displaying these ideas and suggestions, the centre staff networked with families and others in the local community to further develop the ideas. An outcome of this networking was that families and others from the community donated time and skills to construct the stepping stones. The centre also received $500 from a Mitre 10 grant to help fund the stepping stones.

In 2005 the associated artwork in the stepping stone area came to fruition with the assistance of a local art teacher and students from Terrigal High School and a local artist Sharon Tudor. These people visited the centre to hear the children's ideas and look at their drawings and plans. Then, with on-going collaboration, they produced a mural containing a rainbow and aspects of sea life and some sculptures.

Also, a rainwater tank was funded by a local government 'Tanks for Schools' grant and the tank now supplies water for the children's toilets, a water feature and the garden. Local parents assisted to build a fence around the rainwater tank and connect the water feature to the fence.

Further outcomes since the 'Little Green Steps' professional development have included:

- a worm farm and compost bin that the children help to maintain daily;
- a herb and vegetable garden; and
- implementation of water saving strategies (and education of families too).

Playspace features include

- many tall native trees that attract an array of bird species;
- a worm farm and compost bin;
- a rainwater tank;
- a colourful water scene mural painted on the rainwater tank fence;
- a stepping stone garden, each stone decorated with local seashells and coloured stones by the children;
- a 'dinosaur garden' designed and constructed by the children;
- sunshades that blend in with the natural environment;
- several small herb and vegetable garden plots dispersed throughout the playspace;
- shrubs and herbs in large flowerpots that can be moved around the playspace to meet climate changes and conditions (the younger children planted these); and
- two birdbaths that are regularly visited by birds (children use their unwanted water from lunch to top up the birdbaths).

Benefits and outcomes

The natural aesthetics of the playspace are more pleasing and welcoming and at the same time provide opportunities for a sensory-rich experience. In particular, there are opportunities for:

- developing an appreciation and understanding of the natural environment;
- healthy risk taking;
- developing physical fitness;
- planting, tending, collecting and eating organically grown vegetables and herbs;
- developing an awareness of healthy environments; and
- exploring water conservation with children and families.

Goals for the future

- levelling out sloping surfaces to improve opportunities for physical play;
- changing some areas to foster social play; for example, construct a bench seat around a shade tree;
- removing treated pine borders;
- using recycled or re-useable materials for new construction and only purchasing high quality and appropriate materials to meet local climate conditions.

Concerns

During spring the centre has swarms of bees visiting a large flowering shade tree in the middle of the playspace and as a consequence bees do sting children during this period. This is a natural cycle for the bees and the centre can't do much about this. The staff have extended children's knowledge and interest in

Filling the bird bath and emptying scraps into the compost are daily experiences at Terrigal.

bees by developing a bee project around springtime. All staff monitor children who have allergies to bee stings and are vigilant about keeping these children away from this area when required.

Final words of advice for other centres considering a natural playspace

When purchasing plants for natural playspaces consider plants that need minimum water and indigenous plants and always check for potentially poisonous plants. After planting, use a mulch; sugar cane mulch is a good natural mulch and easy to spread. A compost bin, worm farm and birdbath are essential in a natural playspace.

Yirrkala Dhanbul Childcare Preschool Centre

Carmel Gynell—Co-ordinator

Yirrkala is a remote community located on the Gove Peninsula overlooking the Arafura Sea some 800 kilometres east of Darwin, Northern Territory and home to approximately 1000 Indigenous Australians. The Yirrkala Dhanbul Childcare Preschool Centre offers a preschool program for 15 children and childcare for 17 children from the local community. The children range in age from 8 months to 5 years.

Impetus for a natural playspace

A number of factors provided the impetus for change:

- the number of children attending the centre increased in 2004 when the preschool group joined the child care group, hence greater outdoor space was required;

- staff recognised that the layout of the outdoor playspace was somewhat haphazard and did not relate well to the overall function of the centre. It seemed there was no real plan; and
- the local community members were seeking a safe, but adventurous and interesting playspace for children. Also, a space that reflected the local indigenous culture and environment.

The process of change

The process of change began with staff reflecting on the importance of play and identifying play objectives including physical and sensory experience, intellectual growth, creative and dramatic opportunities, language, individuality and social and emotional integration. A safe playspace that also offered challenge and choice was considered essential. The role of the staff in the playspace and how this related to the design was also discussed. After much brainstorming and consultation with the local community, a small-scale three-dimensional design was created. The design incorporated not only the size increase but also the sloping landscape, natural features, existing native vegetation and drainage. Soft fall and grass areas were included and flexibility to meet various play objectives underpinned the design.

The playspace is being developed in stages, as funding becomes available. The builders for the first stage became part of the collaborative process as they worked by day in the playspace alongside the children and staff and then slept at night in the centre.

Playspace features include

- a small wading pool adjacent to the sandpit;
- a water bubbler fountain that spurts from a boulder in the wading pool;
- stepping stones that lead from the lower playspace to the natural bush;
- eight clan poles donated by the local Arts Centre installed in the bush area to promote language skills and reflect local culture;
- a slide sited on a slope embedded with tyres;
- open grassed areas for various play experiences;
- a tanbark soft fall area for climbing equipment;
- a boat embedded in sand as a dramatic play prop and reflecting the coastal location;
- seating made from logs and boulders; and
- a wooden bridge.

Benefits and outcomes

The playspace invites children to freely explore and to be themselves. The playspace reflects their home environment and thus, both promotes and protects their culture and language. The children's input has been valued and a safe, healthy and happy place for children has been created.

Goals for the future

The playspace work will continue for many, many years! Areas needing further work include the hut, the bike shed, more fencing and improved shade.

Final words of advice for other centres considering a natural playspace

- every playspace should be a special place for children. Children of all ages, cultures and abilities have the right to their own special playspaces for them to develop and grow. A natural playspace unwraps new experiences for children, has the potential to excite children's minds and can be changed as children develop;
- always consider the children's needs in designing a natural playspace—a wide variety of safe, but flexible play areas is essential;
- a natural playspace should be realistic and aesthetically inviting, not artificial; and
- all decisions must be community decisions—creating a playspace is a collaborative and consultative process.

International perspectives on natural

playspaces

Joanne Sørensen, Sue Vaealiki, Tracy Young

Introduction

The three international case studies described in this chapter are from Denmark, New Zealand and the United Kingdom. Each case study illustrates a unique perspective on natural outdoor playspaces and invites critical reflection about Australian practices in early childhood playspaces.

To initiate this reflection, questions raised by the case studies could include:

- Why do Australian centres keep children indoors in cooler weather when in Denmark babies sleep outdoors in snowy weather?
- Where is the national United Kingdom school playground support service, Learning Through Landscapes, equivalent in Australia to actively promote improvement in outdoor playspaces?
- How is Indigenous culture embedded in Australian early childhood programs when compared to New Zealand?
- Have our regulatory processes gone too far when compared to the freedoms and risks identified in the Danish case study?

Readers are encouraged read, review, reflect and pose further questions.

Haven Childcare Centre

The Danish Connection: Den Integrerede Institution Haven, Århus, Denmark

Joanne Sørensen

Introduction

The focus of this section is to highlight the culture, philosophy and practices of a Danish childcare centre that have influenced the design and organisation of the outdoor playspace. These elements are interwoven into all aspects of the educational program and impact upon and shape the interactions, attitudes and values of the children.

D.I.I. is the acronym for Den Integrerede Institution meaning that children from birth to 6 years are integrated throughout the centre. Haven directly translates to 'the garden'. The centre opened in 1998 and is a council-run childcare facility located in Århus, the second largest city in Denmark.

D.I.I. Haven is ideally situated in the middle of the city, next to the botanical gardens and within easy access to the local forest and beach. The centre caters for 52 children a day that are divided up into three groups aptly named after regional trees species Beech, Birch and Ash. There are about 18 children in each grouping, often including siblings, under the supervision of two teachers and one assistant. There are several male staff members employed within this centre, as the early childhood field is recognised as a desirable and reasonably well paid career option. All the children who attend are enrolled on a full-time basis, which allows for consistency within the week and they remain in the same group during their time in the centre. Often the children have the same teachers for at least two to three years and build very trusting long-term relationships.

The philosophy

D.I.I. Haven has an underlying philosophy that every individual child should be actively involved in and learn to understand their role in the centre community. The centre also recognises and advocates that the integration and interactions of the differing ages within the groups is the most natural way that children learn and develop their skills. Within the daily program, educators ensure that children are offered flexible play options and react spontaneously to the children's ideas and perspective. They support the children to envisage and realise a range of possibilities and extend the learning in meaningful ways by researching information, seeking resources and organising spontaneous outings.

Throughout the week there are also several planned experiences, such as excursion days where one or more groups can decide to venture out of the centre for the morning. Destinations include the Art Museum, Natural History Museum, Council Library, the park and the shops to purchase any items needed for the program. On these adventures, children catch public transport and there is the flexibility to spend hours observing and investigating the scenery, based on the children's interests. One morning I watched as several children expressed an interest in wanting to further research the topic of birds, so, the teacher took those children to the Museum for the morning to extend their learning. It is an accepted part of Danish childcare culture that all children should have regular opportunities to be part of the local community as much as possible. These occasions happen on a regular basis due to the centre's relatively autonomous self-management, there are very few regulations or requirements.

Another example of the centre's progressive program is that during every spring and autumn, for three days each week over three weeks, the 3–6 year olds visit Hørhaven; a facility which is normally a Scout camp. The children spend the mornings freely exploring a multitude of challenging experiences such as tree climbing, treasure hunts, beach walks, skimming stones over the surface of the ocean, whittling wood with small sharp knives, cooperatively building dams in the small stream with experimental materials, ball sports, navigating the steep hills and cooking on the open fire. Once a year in summer, the staff take these children to the same place again to sleepover for three days and two nights. This holiday occurs without the involvement of parents, who recognise and demonstrate a trusting respect for the judgment and abilities of the educators. This event excites both staff and children alike and is eagerly anticipated every year.

The organisation of the physical environment and the choice of open-ended materials has been arranged to promote play and to focus on the development of a range of skills as well as inspire creativity. This totem pole was part of a larger experience. A few of the older children expressed interest in whittling so a staff member made this totem pole with them during the course of many weeks, inspiring many conversations whilst teaching the children a range of skills.

The lower sandpit area. After several loads of sand were brought in, the centre managed to acquire three very freshly cut trees to plant into the ground. These started growing and have had multiple uses including as supports for hammocks.

The staff advocate for and acknowledge the importance of providing and co-creating a multitude of stimulating spaces for the children's play and ensure ample time is given for children to be involved, make connections and repeat experiences. The organisation of the physical environment and the choice of open-ended materials have been arranged to promote play and to focus on the development of a range of skills as well as inspire creativity. The centre believes that differing types of play form the basis of healthy personal development and that through play children acquire competence, adapt new knowledge and develop confidently at their own pace. The Director of D.I.I. Haven, Vibeke Nielsen explained that play and the development of social competencies has a very high priority throughout the Danish childcare culture.

One of the most significant goals of the centre is that they aim to encourage children to be involved with, value and respect nature. This approach is interwoven into every aspect of the program and philosophy. This connection with nature is an important element that impacts on and shapes the organisation of the physical environment, the structure of the day and the learning experiences that are offered. A direct quote from their philosophy reinforces this inspiring ethos 'Haven is a garden, where children and adults must thrive in beautiful surroundings and be inspired by nature's colours and scents'.

The outdoor playspace—an overview

Creating the framework for the design of the outdoor environment began when the centre was first constructed. Danish regulations once required 10 square metres per child, but this is no longer the case. This centre is very fortunate having a total of 1990 square metres outdoor playspace or 38 square metres per child. Based on their ideas and knowledge, the Director, Vibeke Nielsen, and Assistant Director, Tove Jessen Rasmussen, devised a series of simple sketches of the playspace layout and proposed structures. Their aim was to integrate a range of learning areas that would comfortably harmonise with the local natural surroundings. The learning areas included interconnecting spaces to be creative, social, exert energy, quietly contemplate, actively discover, care for animals and be involved with nature. These areas were then established and since that time there has been a collaborative effort by staff, parents and children to be part of the on-going development process.

Several typical Danish dwellings are represented in the sandpits and are very simply designed to encourage multiple uses.

Over a period of five years, staff, families and children involved with the centre have regularly been given the opportunity to contribute their suggestions and observations. For example, several years ago one staff member's idea was to extend the playspace into an unused car park adjoining the centre. Consultation with the local residents and council then ensured the project occurred and a parent working bee began the process. Over a period of time the space was converted into 'the lower sandpit area'.

Participants have watched the playground continuously evolve based on their needs, ideas and current pedagogical directions. This sense of community involvement is recognised as a valued approach, and has encouraged ownership of the process, further involvement and a sense of achievement.

The Danish are well known for their incredible sense of design and attention to detail, and this is also reflected in early childhood playspaces. Changing with the seasons the large playspace has several specific design features that stimulate all the senses. Aesthetics is a very essential and distinctive component of the centre and great efforts are made to provide materials and spaces that have different forms, shapes, textures and natural colours. The photographs illustrate there is very little use of artificial colour in the playspace, apart perhaps from some of the children's toys.

At Haven it is acknowledged that natural and recycled materials invite children to be inspired, to think of multiple uses and involve themselves in diversely rich creative play episodes. Notice the careful arrangement of seeds, leaves and twigs next to the rock.

The outdoor playspace—specific features

One of the most significant features is the use of natural and or recycled resources. A range of open-ended and portable materials such as sticks, rocks, planks of wood and old tyres are gathered, grouped and arranged for active exploration. The centre's location in the botanical gardens has been very advantageous for sourcing natural items, as the local council workers contribute many of the offcuts that they regularly prune from trees. At this centre it is acknowledged that these materials invite children to be inspired, to think of multiple uses and involve themselves in diversely rich creative play episodes.

Also, after Christmas every year, the children of the centre go to great efforts to collect the old Christmas trees from the surrounding neighbourhood. These discarded trees then become an important focus of the daily play. This movable 'tree' equipment ideally lends itself to the children improvising, organising and being in control of their own play. A sense of ownership for the structures that they have fashioned eventuates as the children continue to build upon their ideas over a period of time. Throughout the morning I observed active conversation between the co-constructors and an adult, which resulted in a cubby arrangement being adjusted and remodelled to include multiple exit and entrance points. When the children decide they have finished interacting with the trees, burning them in the fireplace reuses the trees.

Around the main building there is a large bike track and many children regularly bring their own bikes from home to practise on. Sometimes there are daily bike rides through the botanical gardens, where they may take a packed lunch and venture out for the whole day. Bikes play an important part in Danish culture and for some families this is often their main mode of transport. Denmark is predominantly flat and the road system has been specially designed to provide for large and very safe bike paths along all roads.

A special bench to whittle wood is also a feature. To make their designs, the younger children use a vegetable peeler, whilst the older more capable children use small sharp knives. The leftover shavings are then used to fuel the fire.

There are two sandpits of different sizes that are used for different purposes. The larger sandpit is bottomless, so the children can dig as long and deep as they like. Several typical Danish dwellings are represented in the sand pit area and are very simply designed to encourage multiple uses.

The design of this large log invites a range of open-ended uses.

A variety of garden areas that are used for many purposes cover the landscape. Several trees have bird boxes nestled high up in their branches and closely planted shrubs provide many possibilities to hide and be at peace. There is a large grassy area with undulating terrain and fragrant planting, which has space to hang several restful hammocks.

A green house and raised garden beds are situated close to the main building. This provides easy access for the children and kitchen staff to use the assortment of seasonal vegetables in their daily meals or cooking experiences. There are also bushes with berries (blackberries, raspberries and elderberries) and fruit trees (apples and plums), herbs and a range of flowers. The centre usually grows a significant number of flowers, so that the children can pick bunches to use in their play or arrange and display them in vases for ornamental purposes. Notably, the centre is also pesticide free and as organic as possible, so that the variety of vegetation in the playspace is edible, which makes it safe for the younger babies and children to be as explorative as they like.

Water conservation is also a feature, as several large wooden kegs stand beside the main building to collect rain water which the children can use in their play and to water the garden.

Extending and reinforcing their role in the community, residents are welcome to use the playspace on the weekends (as there are no external locks on the gates), with the only request that the users tidy up after themselves. This is evident during autumn when locals come over to the playspace to pick the ripe cranberries.

A large chicken coop and guinea pig cage is positioned near the front entrance, as the centre considers that caring for animals is an important and essential learning experience. Children become meaningfully engaged in the maintenance and feeding, through collecting and distributing vegetable scraps from the kitchen. Also, gathering eggs promotes opportunities for cooking and learning about the life cycle of these animals.

Within the design of the playspace there are also quite a few *physically challenging areas* such as uneven hilly areas, knotted ropes to climb steep embankments, a slippery slide, see saws and stairs with no hand rails (where even the smallest children learn to back down and crawl up). A small soccer field supports various physical games.

A unique feature of playspaces in Scandinavian countries is a fireplace, which is often used, especially during spring and autumn. Under the watchful guidance of two adults, children practise being responsible around the fireplace and learn about how to safely use it. Snobrød (similar to damper) is wound around long sticks and dangled at the edge of the fire until it is brown and golden. It's quite a challenge for some children to hold the stick just above the embers so that it doesn't catch fire. Butter and homemade jam from the centre's produce is then smothered onto this favourite treat. To extend on the children's interests, special pans were bought with long handles so that they could safely cook pancakes and a large metal basket is watched intensely when it is used to cook hot popped corn—yum.

Educators value the learning that occurs throughout the year and encourage the children to explore outdoors in all weather conditions. There is a rule that the children must get fresh air and play outside everyday, regardless of the weather, even if it is just for a short period of time. Parents are very supportive of this arrangement and ensure that they provide a range of suitable clothing. Dependent on the season, children are often outside all day, perhaps having a treasure hunt at

A unique feature of playspaces in Scandinavian countries is a fireplace, which is often used, especially during spring and autumn.

Babies and young children sleep outside in all weather conditions, except perhaps a snow storm, until they are too big for the specially designed cots. This practice is well accepted as having great health benefits.

the beach, building a cubby in the local forest over a period of several days or tobogganing in the snow. If the weather is too inclement they then may decide to visit a museum or art gallery. Somewhat incredibly, babies and young children sleep outside in all weather conditions, except perhaps a snow storm, until they are too big for the specially designed cots. This practice is well accepted as having great health benefits

Conclusion

D.I.I. Haven provides an example of an inspirational collaborative learning journey in the early childhood years, not only for the children but also the staff and parents. The outdoor playspace and supporting philosophy creates a diverse range of opportunities for interaction and learning with natural materials, plants, animals and the elements. What can we learn from the experiences at Haven and how can we translate them into practice?

Acknowledgment

Many thanks to all the staff, children and parents of Haven who agreed to participate and share with us, the culture of their dynamic early childhood centre.

References

D.I.I. Haven website (in Danish):http://portal.aarhus-m1.dk/htm/inst.php?pasnr=1008&page=1.
OECD (from 2001) document about early childhood centres in Denmark: http://www.oecd.org/dataoecd/31/56/33685537.pdf.

Weaving 'our cultural, social and environmental identity' into outdoor playspaces: some thoughts from New Zealand

Sue Vaealiki

Introduction

Aotearoa/New Zealand, is a land of beautiful islands which span 1600 kilometres from Cape Reinga to Stewart Island. The mountain ranges that form the backbone of the two main islands are a stunning backdrop to the diverse landscapes and a unique ecology. Māori, the *tangata whenua* (people of the land), were the first to make New Zealand their home and during the last two centuries people from around the world and the Pacific regions have settled here to create a nation of many cultures. Surrounded by the natural beauty of the land and the sea it has been easy to take for granted the opportunities for young children to connect with the natural world. But, like most societies, New Zealand is affected by the rapid social, economic, technological and environmental changes occurring across the world. With the increased urbanisation of families and the growth of cities in New Zealand, children's access to safe, open playspaces has decreased. For this reason, many early childhood teachers in New Zealand are re-evaluating the playspaces provided in their centres, so that there are increased opportunities for children to deepen their connections and understanding of natural environments.

In recent initiatives undertaken in a nursery and two kindergartens in Christchurch, a South Island city, the teachers have created playspaces that reflect the weaving together of New Zealand's distinctive cultural, social and environmental identity. Guided by *Te Whāriki*, the New Zealand early childhood curriculum, the teachers have initiated these changes by responding to children's interests and ideas, and fostering partnerships with parents and the local community. Underpinning the teachers' work are the four principles of *Te Whāriki*:

1. empowerment—whakamana;
2. holistic development—kotahitanga;
3. family and community—whānau tangata; and
4. relationships—ngā hononga.

Each of these principles reflects the importance of reciprocal, responsive relationships between the teacher, the child and the family. Embedded in the framework is an environmental focus found in the strands of *'mana whenua'* (belonging), and *'mana aotūroa'* (exploration); both these strands include the importance of the child knowing, caring and developing a relationship with the natural world.

Mana whenua

If an environmental lens is placed on the concept of 'mana whenua', children's knowledge of their place in the world, their spiritual and physical connections with significant local features such as the rivers and mountains, and their skills to care for these places have a strong focus in the early childhood centre. This concept involves creating a sense of belonging and developing meaningful relationships with the families, so that they share their aspirations and participate collaboratively in decisions related to their child's learning. The following paragraphs and photographs provide a glimpse of the changes that the teachers,

Investigating the local landscape through maps and photographs at Kidsfirst Lincoln Kindergarten.

Children's creative responses to exploring the local landscape at Kidsfirst Lincoln Kindergarten.

Making a plan for the new garden at Kidsfirst Lincoln Kindergarten.

Debbie and Dawn, facilitated in the outdoor playspace of the infant and toddler nursery at 'New Beginnings'. These changes reflect a way to integrate the concept of 'mana whenua'.

New Beginnings: Transforming the infants and toddlers outdoor playspace

The transformation of the outdoor playspace began with a small research project that led to the teachers replacing plastic play materials with natural materials. As this happened, the parents began to share their childhood memories of their outdoor playspaces and through discussion a shared vision and aspiration for the children developed. Debbie noted:

> We all have special childhood memories of playing in nature and through sharing these ideas we could strengthen our connections and relationships with each other. We took a lot of care to observe and think about what the infants and toddlers needed, to climb, to move. As we shared what we were noticing through learning stories, the parents responded back with what they were also noticing about their children's interest in nature.

As the design of the new outdoor environment began to take shape, the parents' commitment and involvement in the project enabled the creation of a unique outdoor playspace that represented their aspirations for their children. Together with the teachers, parents gave time, resources and energy to creating a playspace that used native plants, wood, stone, sand and water to present challenges and exploration for the infants and toddlers. The plants and stones were arranged in symbolic patterns that have cultural meaning for the families; koru (spirals) take centre place. It also offered quiet spaces where infants and toddlers take a pause from the busyness of their play. Dawn reflects on the changes thus:

> … we have created a play environment where things are slowed right down, where children notice the natural world and experience it through all their senses. We are becoming more flexible as teachers, letting go of some of our routines and letting children make choices about the different ways to experience the world. Our interactions with the infants and toddlers have become deeper and more open-ended.

Mana aotūrua

This strand in *Te Whāriki* emphasises that children's active exploration in nature strengthens their relationship, knowledge and respect for the natural environment. In addition, teachers can empower children to develop skills to protect the environment by helping children to investigate, problem solve and theorise about their experiences. It is especially important that children are provided with a variety of ways to explain and express these ideas including creative media, technology, music and drama. The following accounts are of two kindergartens attended by children between the ages of 3 and 5 years and illustrate the active exploration inspired by *mana aotūroa*.

'Tūrangawaewae'

At Kidsfirst Kindergarten in Lincoln a project called '*Tūrangawaewae*' has led to the teachers, Nicky, Birgit and Jeanne, creating a cultural garden with the children and parents. '*Tūrangawaewae*' is a Māori concept that literally means the place you have a right to 'stand on'. It embodies the idea that a person's identity is deeply linked to the place they belong to and with this comes '*kaitiakitanga*', the responsibility to protect the 'mauri', the life force of this place (http://en.wikipedia.org/wiki).

The project began with the 4-year olds coming to know about the rivers and mountains close to their community. Nicky describes their approach thus 'this year we have taken the children back to looking at their roots, their place in the world, their uniqueness. We have encouraged children to express their ideas through art and in their play'.

A field trip into the hills so that the children could see over the Canterbury Plains allowed the children to visually see how the landscape was connected with mountains and rivers. Birgit describes how the children brought this play back into the sandpit where they built models of the plains capturing the interconnectedness of the landscape. As the children's understanding of and fascination with their surrounding landscapes grew, they expressed a desire to create a garden that represented their cultural understandings of themselves. The garden has since become a focal point in the centre and flourishes with the care that the children, teachers and parents lavish on it. Jeanne notes that each child chose to be involved in ways that they could express themselves best; landscape artists, concrete makers, gardeners and, most importantly of all, guardians for their environment. 'Some children have been particularly interested in producing designs for the shape of the garden, others in the construction of the paths and edges and some in the physical work of caring for the plants.'

Birgit noticed that the children related more easily to environmental issues when the issues had relevance in their lives. As the kindergarten is situated in a farming community, the topics of water and irrigation were frequently discussed around the kitchen table. Now that the next project at the kindergarten is to investigate water conservation, children are bringing their prior knowledge to these experiences and discussing their ideas at home.

The finished garden at Kidsfirst Lincoln Kindergarten, note the symbolic fern fiddle head design made from stones embedded in concrete.

Rosie at the local community garden, a collaborative effort.

Many early childhood teachers may regard this investigation as too complex for the 4-year-old child. 'Not so', says Nicky, 'integrating environmental projects that relate to children's use of the playspaces has been an empowering experience for both the staff and the children. We see the expertise that children bring to these projects, the way they care for the environment, inspires their parents and us. We are listening much more carefully to their ideas.'

Scarecrows and the 'not to be' herb garden

Rose the scarecrow sits with pride of place in the local community gardens in Opawa. Named by the children who created her at Kidsfirst Kindergarten Opawa, she is the result of the children's knowledge and interest in environmentally friendly gardening. In the last two years, the children and teachers, Maggie, Robyn, Jo and Ruth, have been involved in a number of environmental projects and now the kindergarten integrates recycling, composting, worm farming and gardening into the daily curriculum.

The teachers, parents and children, through a mutual interest in caring for the environment, have fostered the partnership between the kindergarten and the community garden co-ordinator. Regular visits to the gardens through all the seasons have maintained this partnership. Maggie notes that 'we have truly developed a reciprocal partnership. When the old tan bark was due for renewal in our playspace we were able to take it to the community gardens for recycling. The children have made birdfeeders for the gardens and with such spectacular results we are now in the business of making scarecrows!'

Robyn comments that:

> … our relationship with the community gardens has been very positive. Firstly, it created a greater sense of ownership and pride in the gardens at the kindergarten. Secondly, children's interest in gardening is inspiring parents to visit the community gardens. We now have our own plot down there and parents and children visit this in the weekend.

The children's involvement in the community gardens demonstrates that young children are citizens who enjoy and can competently contribute to the social and environmental sustainability of their communities. However, this can only be fully realised if adults step back and take time to listen to children's viewpoints. Maggie reflects about the process of developing the 'not to be' herb garden by the sandpit:

> All of us adults thought that this was the ideal place for a herb garden, but when the children were consulted they only wanted flowers. Suddenly, we realised that we had been really good at suggesting our ideas to the children and then spending a lot of time convincing them that this was the best idea! But, this time the children clearly told us the herb garden was 'not to be'. So thinking a lot more about the principles of 'genuine participation' and empowerment we set about gathering the children's ideas. Plenty of paper and crayons were put out the next day and the children came up with lots of suggestions for the colour and the type of flowers they wanted. This has led to a deeper investigation of what will grow well in this area. With the help of one of our grandmothers who belongs to a gardening club the children are now in the process of making the final selection.

Conclusion

Each centre described above has developed their outdoor playspaces in unique ways. The teachers have shown that the development of playspaces is enriched when we make visible the children's voices and the aspirations of their parents. Critical to the success of these projects has been the importance of working with children, their families and the local community so that the playspaces reflect the interweaving of the social, cultural and environmental identity of each community. An expression of these ideas is found in the following Māori *whakataukī*

Manaaki whenua Care for the land
Manaaki tangata Care for the people
Haere whakamua Go forward
(http://www.landcareresearch.co.nz/publications)

References

Ministry of Education, 1996, *Te Whāriki; He Whāriki Mātauranga Mō Ngā Mokopuna o Aotearoa; Early childhood curriculum*, Learning Media, Wellington.
http://www.landcareresearch.co.nz/publications Retrieved 22/10/05 from http://en.wikipedia.org/wiki.

Acknowledgment

I would like to thank the teachers, children and parents from New Beginnings Nursery, Kidsfirst Kindergartens Opawa and Lincoln for allowing me to share their stories and photos. A special thanks to Diane Gordon-Burns of Ngaati Mahuta for her guidance on aspects of Te Ao Māori.

Learning through Landscapes UK

Tracy Young

Introduction

Since 1990, Learning through Landscapes (LTL) has been campaigning on behalf of all children for better school grounds from early childhood to high school. They believe that school grounds play a vital role in a child's learning and development. Playgrounds are essential and unique spaces, providing diverse opportunities for understanding, achievement and attainment and for healthy exercise and creative play. They believe that children and young people who do not have access to good school grounds are missing out on the best start in life.

LTL is a national school grounds charity and provides a support service to help schools develop grounds that are well used, enjoyed and valued by the whole school community. LTL also focuses on giving children and young people a say in the way these spaces are used and improved. They have approximately 7000 members who work with the early childhood years. The British government in 2002 introduced compulsory guidelines for outside play for the early years curriculum (foundation stage 3–5 years) and this has been significant in promoting the value of outdoor play.

LTL has made connections in Australia through the Gould League in Victoria, The School Landscapes Trust and the Brungle School in New South Wales that are featured on the LTL website. Worldwide connections include several schools in South Africa, New Zealand, USA and Canada. Also, LTL has been working on a project involving schools in Sweden and the UK with the Swedish organisation Barnens Lanskpap (Children's Landscape). The eminent naturalist Sir David Attenborough is one of the organisation's patrons. LTL has a number of videos and publications, membership (including overseas membership) opportunities and a very useful website.

Some of the benefits of developing outside spaces were highlighted in a recent LTL survey (2003) of 700 British schools and early years settings that have improved their outdoor spaces with the support of LTL. The survey indicated:

- 73 per cent have seen improved pupil behaviour;
- 64 per cent have seen reductions in bullying;
- 65 per cent have seen attitudes towards learning improved;
- 84 per cent have seen better social interaction; and
- 66 per cent say school grounds improvements increase community/ parental involvement.

These outcomes demonstrate that investment in outdoor playspaces is not just about outdoor play per se, but a range of positive outcomes for children, families and communities. Other researchers such as Stephen Kellert, who makes a strong point about the apparent decline of children's direct exposure to natural environments, also support this. Kellert concludes 'that the child's direct and ongoing experience of accessible nature is an essential, critical and irreplaceable dimension of healthy maturation and development' (Kahn and Kellert, 2002, p xiii).

The Coombes County Infant and Nursery School, Berkshire

On a glorious warm day in July 2005, I was privileged to visit The Coombes School in Berkshire that incorporates nursery, infant, junior and senior schools with children and young adults aged between 3 and 18 years. The school has won many awards including The European School of the year in 1996.

The school meets the requirements of the National Curriculum, but goes beyond this focus by offering a team of experiences that anchor education in the real world. The school attracts visitors from all over Britain and overseas who come to observe the innovative and imaginative teaching methods.

I was warmly welcomed at the school by Sue Humphries, the retired head of the school who still plays an active role. Sue Rowe is the current head of the school and both Sues have co-authored books about science. I realised from the start that this was an unusual situation for what can only be described as a unique school. Sue suggested that two children show me around and point out some of their favourite places in the schoolgrounds. I set off with Oliver

The Coombes' sheep sheltering from an English summer day.

Rules for looking after sheep and lambs

1. Keep them warm
2. feed them
3. Make them healthy
4. give them Shelter
5. feed them milk
6. Keep them comfy
7. Shear them every Summer

Children are actively involved in caring for the sheep along with other experiences that anchor education in the real world.

Model of London Town made with recycled materials such as cardboard boxes.

Further examples of an active approach to learning. The children were exploring force and flight in these photographs.

and Zenovia, both six years of age and eager to share their knowledge and wisdom. It quickly became evident these children were able to impart incredible insight into many aspects of the school grounds, not only the natural science components, but also how history, art, physics, geology, geography and social studies are explored through the natural environment.

The inclusion of real life experiences for teaching and learning in the school is evident in both the inside and outside environments. Many of these real life experiences are linked to not only the immediate school community, but also the wider community. For example, the small herd of sheep that are kept at the school. The children have the opportunity to find out about the life cycle of these mammals, how the birth of lambs fits with the seasons and how to care for sheep. The children chose names for the lambs. They also observed

The school uses a lot of willow, a versatile and renewable resource that can be used in a variety of ways. Cut stakes pushed into the right sort of ground will take root and grow. Some of the archways made by growing willow are shown.

We study life and death

This deer was killed by a car.
We brought it to school.

Photo of the deer on school noticeboard.

traditional skills such as sheep shearing at close hand and worked with the fleece to make felt, weave and dye with natural dyes they had made themselves. A local shearer shears the sheep each year and the children participate in this experience.

The teaching is committed to an active education philosophy based on the belief that if a child has participated with their whole body in a learning experience, they are more likely to remember it and absorb its value on a number of levels. The school seeks to develop the immeasurable, not just the parts of education that can be easily labelled, tested and accounted for. Some photographs displayed in the school entrance demonstrated an example of this active learning approach. The children had been exploring the history of the great fire of London and had built a large-scale model of this from cardboard boxes. This large recreation of London was taken outside where it was set fire, with the fire originating from a bakery in Pudding Lane.

The grounds of the school include planted woodlands, several ponds, glades of bluebells and other spring bulbs, compost bins, multiple vegetable gardens and fruit trees. An arboretum has been designed to include representative samples of all trees found in Northern Europe. There are many willow trees and their branches were used for archways or bowers that created interesting doorways and structures for children to explore. Woven into the natural playground are challenging and interesting structures to investigate such as tree houses, a viewing platform, tunnels, a bridge, boardwalks and hard and soft surfaces. There is also a geology trail including their own Stonehenge called 'Coombeshenge' and other massive stones brought in to represent the geological regions of the British Isles.

There were two examples during my visit that highlighted the school's willingness to explore contentious issues such as life and death and the interconnectedness of plants, animals and people in the natural world:

- The children showed me where a dead fox had been found under a bridge. The teachers had buried the fox and then dug it up some weeks later to examine the bones. Both children expressed detailed knowledge about what may have happened to the fox and expressed how interesting it was to look at the bones, 'like the bones in my body'.
- The second example is outlined in the photograph above. A young deer was knocked down and killed outside the school, as the children were arriving one morning. One of the parents brought the deer inside and many children examined the body. The deer was not externally damaged, so it was decided that this would not be too graphic for young children. One of the grandparents buried the deer, but not before the whole school was involved in discussion about life and death.

This type of subject material is often avoided with children for fear that it will upset them or open up a world of reality that they may not ready to cope with. The Coombes School involves children and families in this discussion and is sometimes criticised or misunderstood for this approach. One of the teachers stated that they are sometimes referred to 'as that school where you examine road kill'.

Another feature of the school is the use of maps and boundaries to construct knowledge of spatial dimensions and geography. The children in the mixed age group classroom, aged 5, 6 and 7 years that I observed, highlighted their favourite features in the outside space. The teacher regularly included map work and this was extended by one of the rituals of the school, called 'Beating of the Grounds' where the perimeters of the school are beaten by the children with a large stick to facilitate their understanding of the dimensions of space. The grounds have a number of pathways that combine to create over a kilometre of interconnecting pathways. Each pathway has different start and finish points and different textures underfoot from the hard concrete to the springier texture of the bark-chipping pathway. Where the pathways have overhanging trees they are managed so that the walkways are child height, adults must bend! The pathways offer light and dark, shade or open sky, colours, textures and patterns. They connect one interesting feature to another.

Oliver and Zenovia standing under Coombeshenge.

Large compost bins are used with children actively involved in the process of producing compost.

These vegetables are grown with a drip irrigation system that explores simple physics.

The natural world is explored on a regular basis at the school not only through the aesthetically appealing natural surroundings, but also through sustainable practices and a deep commitment to the interconnectedness of natural systems. A range of plants, fruit trees and vegetables are grown and eaten, all supported by large compost systems and sustainable growing techniques. The school also plants many trees and at Christmas, for each cypress tree cut down and decorated, the school plants two more trees.

Since the school opened in 1971, the grounds have been changed, improved and developed. The school is now nationally and internationally recognised as a pioneer and leader in environmental education, playground development and the whole curriculum use of landscapes for learning. I left the school feeling inspired, with an increased awareness that committed teachers who work in partnership with communities, can indeed manifest visions of excellence into actual programs. Outside playspaces can be created that not only inspire children to construct knowledge, but also discover the beauty of the world they live in:

> My favourite things I like to do are going down the pathway to the bluebell wood. I don't like the dog who barks ... I know that the granite that was carved comes from Scotland. The sculpture could not be finished because it started to rain so we have only half a face (*Oliver aged six years*).

References

Kahn PH and Kellert SR, 2002, *Children and Nature*, MIT Press, Massachusetts.
Learning Through Landscapes website http://www.ltl.org.uk.

Bibliography

The Coombes School website http://www.thecoombes.com/frames.html.
The School Landscapes Trust, Australia www.learnscapes.org/.
New Zealand Enviroschools www.enviroschoolsorg.nz.
San Francisco Schoolyard Initiative www.schoolyards.org/.
Barnens Landscap Organisation (translated meaning children's landscape) http://www.barnenslandskap.com/default.asp?lan=eng.

Conclusion

The preparation of this publication has been a shared journey for the editor and chapter authors, a journey that has reaffirmed our commitment to natural play-spaces. As we have progressed on this journey, a number of media reports have highlighted our concerns and, thus, we believe this publication is very timely. Our aim to instigate a paradigm shift from generic, synthetic outdoor playspaces to natural outdoor playspaces for young children is now more urgent than ever.

We trust that the reader has now also experienced a journey—a journey of awakening to the potential of natural playspaces in all respects. Natural playspaces are more than just a few scattered rocks and logs, they are spaces created through a shared vision and collaborative effort, spaces with which children, staff and families identify and spaces that promote engaging and diverse play for all. Hopefully this journey has involved reflection on one's own childhood and connections with the natural environment. The journey may have been challenging, perhaps uncomfortable, but worthwhile in terms of the potential outcomes for early childhood centre playspaces. As the current generation of early childhood educators ages and the younger generation moves forward, there is a concern that the passions for outdoor play with natural materials has diminished already. Do early childhood educators entering the field now have the 'radioactive jewels' (Chawla, 1990, p 18) to draw on to create engaging natural playspaces for young children? Also, overlaying this question is concern about how regulatory authorities are working to promote or deny opportunities to create natural playspaces in early childhood services.

We urge regulatory authorities, managers, designers, parents, committees of management and early childhood educators to reflect deeply on the types of outdoor play experiences that are most beneficial to young children and how these can be promoted in a natural playspace. Also, to reflect on why such playspaces are fundamental to the bigger picture of sustainability. Without the establishment of connections with nature and the nurturing of nature trusting relationships, the potential outcomes of education for sustainabiity programs are thwarted and our very survival on this planet in jeopardy.

References

Chawla L, 1990, 'Ecstatic Places', *Children's Environments Quarterly*, 7(4) pp 18–23.

References
and resources

Bagot K, 2005, 'The Importance of Green Play Spaces for Children—aesthetic, athletic and academic', *Eingana*, Vol 28 No 3, pp 11–15.

Carson R, 1956 republished 1998, *The Sense of Wonder*, Harper Collins Publishers Inc., New York.

Crook S (Ed), 2004, *Just Improvise: Innovative Play Experiences for Children Under Eight*, Tertiary Press, Melbourne.

Commonwealth of Australia Department of Environment and Heritage, 2005, *Education for a Sustainable Future: A National Environmental Education Statement for Schools*, Curriculum Corporation, Carlton.

Commonwealth of Australia Department of Environment and Heritage, 2000, *Environmental Education for a Sustainable Future: National Action Plan*, Department of Environment and Heritage, Canberra.

Davis J, Gibson M, Pratt R, Eglington A and Rowntree N, 2005, 'Creating a culture of sustainability: From project to integrated education for sustainability at Campus Kindergarten', in the *International Handbook of Sustainability Research*, UNESCO, Paris.

Davis J, 2005, 'Education for sustainability in the Early Years: Creating Culture Change in a Child Care Setting' *Australian Journal of Environmental Education*, Vol 21, pp 7–55.

Davis J and Pratt R, 2005, 'Creating culture change at Campus Kindergarten The Sustainable Planet Project', *Everychild*, Vol 11 No 4, pp 10–11.

Elliott S and Emmett S, 1997, *Snails Live in Houses Too, Environmental Education for the Early* Years 2nd edn, RMIT Publications, Melbourne.

EEEC Vic Inc, 1999, *Weaving Webs An Approach to Environmental Education for Young Children*, EEEC Vic. Inc. and Generations Productions, Melbourne.

EEEC Vic Inc, 2003, *EEEC Vic Inc Resource Book*, EEEC Vic Inc, Moonee Ponds.

KU Children's Services, 2004, *KU Environment Policy*, KU Children's Services, Sydney.

Lester S and Maudsley M, 2006, *Play Naturally: A Review of Children's Natural Play*, retrieved 12/06/07 from www.playday.org.uk.

NSW EPA, 2003, *Patches of Green: A Review of Early Childhood Environmental Education*, NSW EPA, Sydney.

Nuttall C, 1996, *A Children's Food Forest*, FeFL Books, Brisbane.

Royal Botanic Gardens, 2003, *Early Childhood Resource Book*, Royal Botanic Gardens, Melbourne.

Sobel D, 2004, *Place-based Education: Connecting Classrooms and Communities*, The Orion Society, Great Barrington, MA.

Sobel D, 1996, *Beyond Ecophobia, Reclaiming the Heart in Nature Education*, The Orion Insitute and The Myrin Institute, Great Barrington, MA.

Tilbury D, Coleman V and Garlick D, 2005, *A National Review of Environmental Education and its contribution to sustainability in Australia: School Education*, Australian Government Department of the Environment and Heritage and Australian Research Institute in Education for Sustainability, Canberra.

UNESCO, 2005, *Decade of Education for Sustainable Development 2005–2014 Draft International Implementation Scheme*, UNESCO, Paris.

Wilson R (Ed), 1994, *Environmental Education at the Early Childhood Level*, NAAEE, Troy, Ohio.

Useful websites

www.rite.ed.qut.edu.au/qeceen/
Queensland Early Childhood Environmental Education Network Inc., a membership-based support and resource organisation that provides regular meetings and newsletters for early childhood services.

http://home.vicnet.net.au/~eeec/
Environmental Education in Early Childhood Vic. Inc., a membership-based support and resource organisation in Melbourne that provides regular meetings, professional development, newsletters and play materials for sale to early childhood services.

www.earlychildhoodaustralia.org.au/nsw_branch/eceen.html
NSW Early Childhood Environmental Education Network auspiced by ECA in NSW provides regular meetings, newsletters and resource kits available for loan.

www.whitehutchinson.com/children/articles/biophilia.shtml
White Hutchinson Leisure & Learning Group has a number of relevant articles including 'Moving from Biophobia to Biophilia: Developmentally Appropriate Environmental Education for Children' by Randy White.

www.ecoinstitute.org/atei.html
The Early Childhood Outdoors Institute or ECO Institute provides a national model (USA) of environmental education for children ages 2–6 years with a focus on nature-based preschools.

www.aaee.org.au
Australian Association for Environmental Education including a national Early Childhood Special Interest Group (AAEE EC SIG) that circulates regular newsletters and connects interested early childhood educators across Australia.

http://portal.unesco.org/education/en/ev.php-URL_ID=27234&URL_DO= DO_TOPIC&URL_SECTION=201.html
UN Decade of Education for Sustainable Development 2005–2014 is currently underway internationally and relevant documents are available from this website.

www.ceres.org.au
Centre for Education and Research into Environmental Strategies (CERES) is an urban community environment park in Melbourne demonstrating a range of sustainable practices. CERES also provides horticultural services including design, consultation and construction for schools and early childhood services. The focus is on sustainable outdoor classrooms.

www.cnaturenet.org
The Children and Nature Network, USA, has been established to champion the causes of Louv's (2005) publication 'The Last Child in the Woods: Saving Our Children from Nature Deficit Disorder'. This network has launched an international movement under the banner 'No Child Left Inside' and provides regular newsletters to facilitate collaborative action and information sharing.

www.ipaworld.org
This international organisation aims to protect, preserve and promote the child's right to play as a fundamental human right. IPA's world wide network promotes the importance of play in child development, provides a vehicle for inter-disciplinary exchange and action, and brings a child perspective to policy development throughout the world.

< 210 >   The Outdoor Playspace Naturally

Index